Life in **five seconds**

OVER 200 STORIES FOR THOSE WITH NO TIME TO WASTE

Life in five seconds

OVER 200 STORIES FOR THOSE WITH NO TIME TO WASTE

Matteo Civaschi   H-57*   Gianmarco Milesi

THE STORY OF THESE STORIES

There's no place for a long introduction in a book called *Life in Five Seconds.*

So here's a short one.

This book is about all of life (from famous people, historic moments and iconic places to little everyday things like pizza) but with the useless and boring parts stripped away.

It's the apple pie without having to peel the apples.
Cats without scooping the litter.
Kissing on the beach, under the moonlight, without sand in awkward places.
Rome without traffic.
Shampoo without tears.
Gravy without splashes down your T-shirt.
Eternal love without the snoring.

You get the picture.
Happy reading!

How to use this book

You could read this book on your own, front to back, like a regular book. A better way is to look at each story and then try to guess the subject without looking at the answers. But the best way – and trust us on this because we tried it for ourselves – is to gather your friends and all guess together. After all, a dozen brains are better than one (except when you have to choose a restaurant!).

How not to use this book

What you absolutely shouldn't do is to use this book as a completely reliable historical and biographical reference, particularly if you're somebody's Phone-A-Friend on *Who Wants to Be a Millionaire*.

Our stories, though generally accurate in terms of chronology, aren't always a precise illustration of what actually happened. Sometimes we improvise. Sometimes we base our story on "we think it went like this" or "we believe they were thinking that", such as Picasso, Freud, Sahara, Atlantis, Everest and the Holy Grail. So, don't necessarily expect historical accuracy. We can't always promise it.

With other stories we illustrate only one aspect or just one part of the timeline (see Jimi Hendrix, John McEnroe and John Paul II). The moments we choose to show may seem minor but are – in our opinion – usually quite significant or revealing.

Be prepared that some stories may be more difficult to decipher than others. Some are

built like quizzes (including Woody Allen, Alfred Hitchcock and *The Simpsons*), with each icon part of the riddle, whilst the book is also dotted here and there with a few lesser-known gems. In both cases, hardcore fans will guess everything immediately, while others may have to do a bit of research. This is all part of the fun. We discovered lots of interesting and curious things whilst creating this book and we hope that you will, too.

A final note: we've tried not to let moral opinions or judgments colour our stories. Not because we don't have these opinions but because we want to let you form your own. Every reader will draw his own conclusions. That said, some people or events do come with inevitable connotations (whether good or bad) that don't need to be underlined.

Now that's really everything.
Enjoy the book!

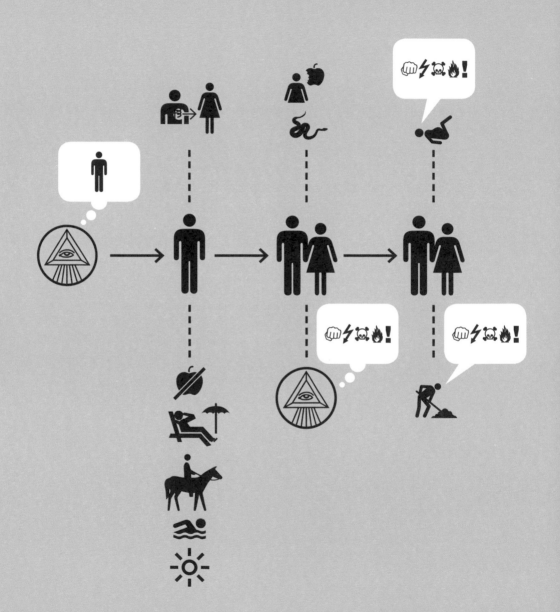

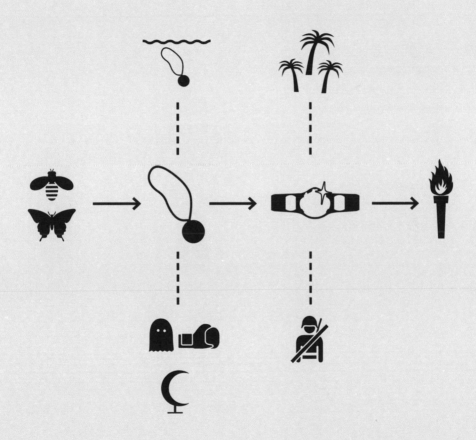

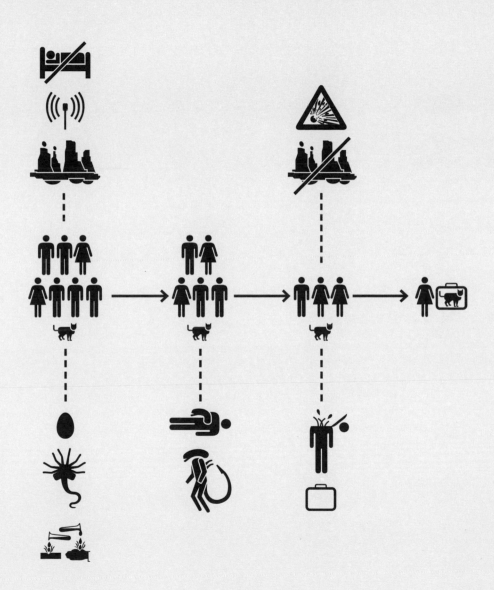

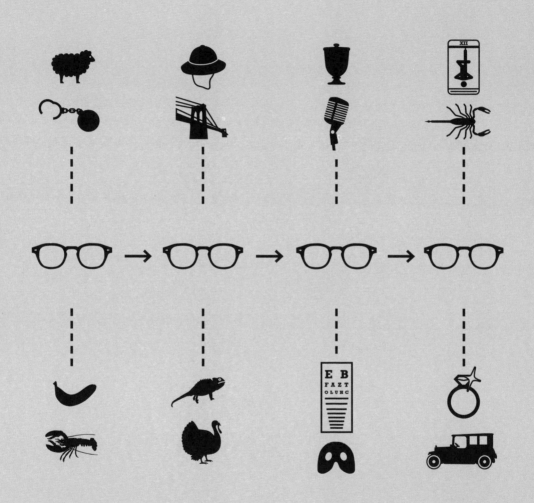

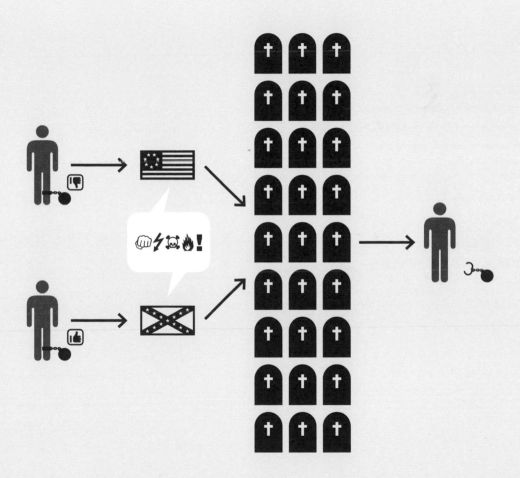

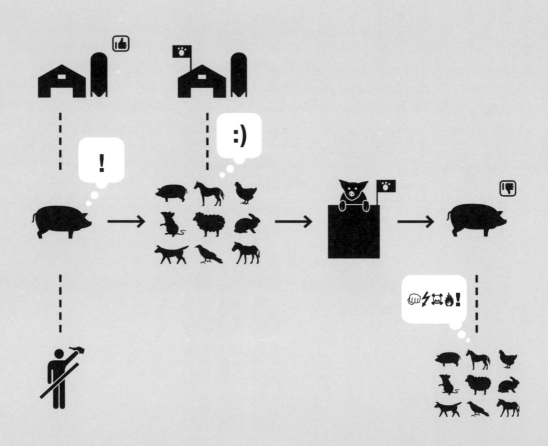

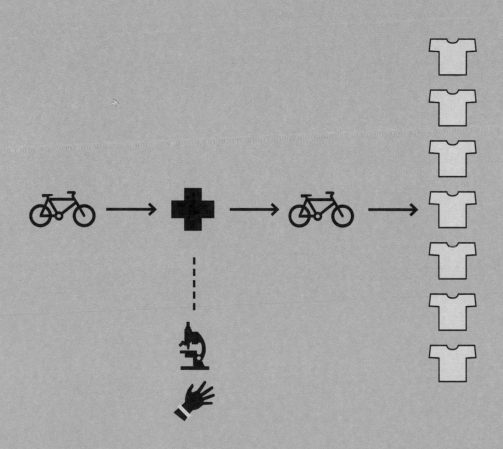

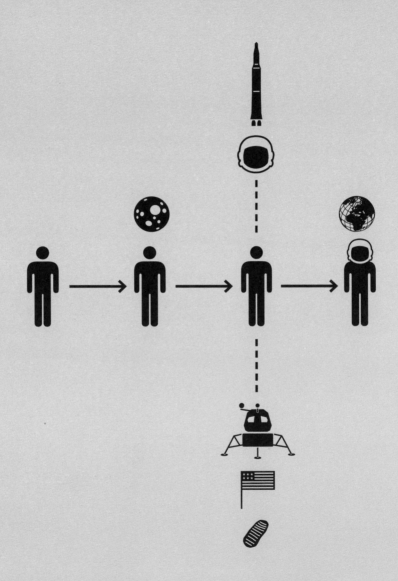

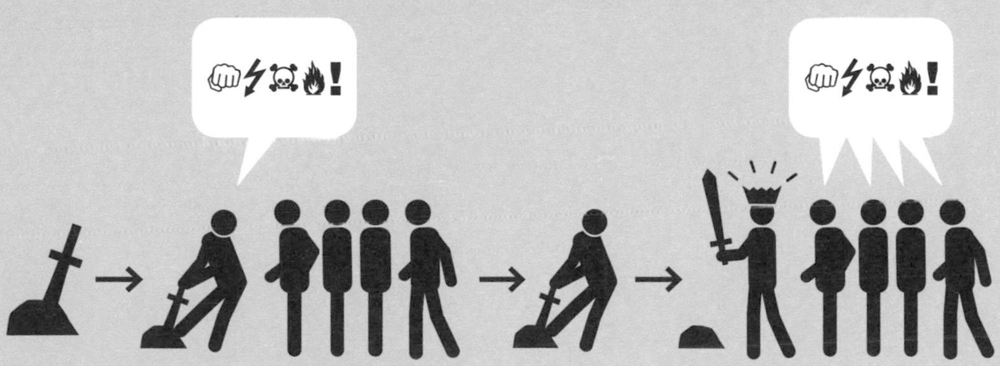

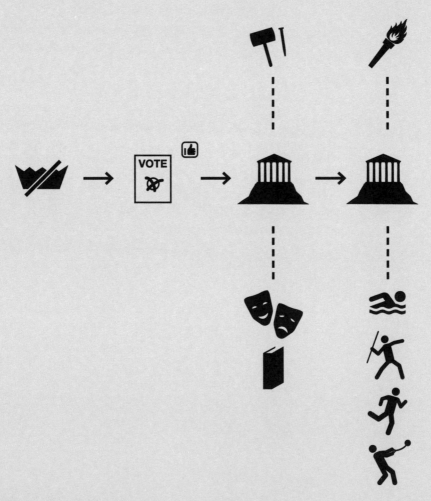

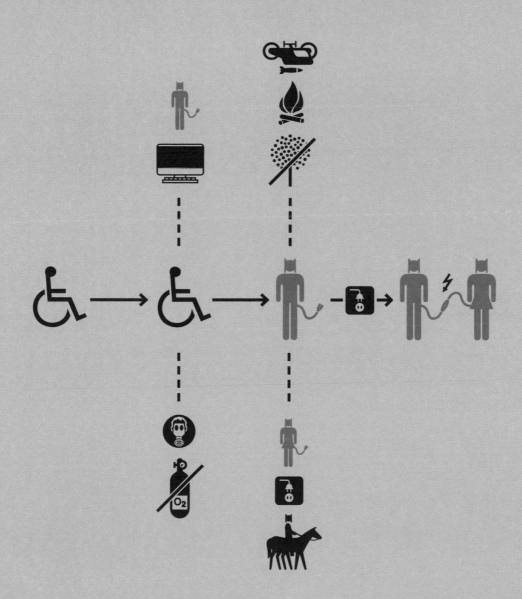

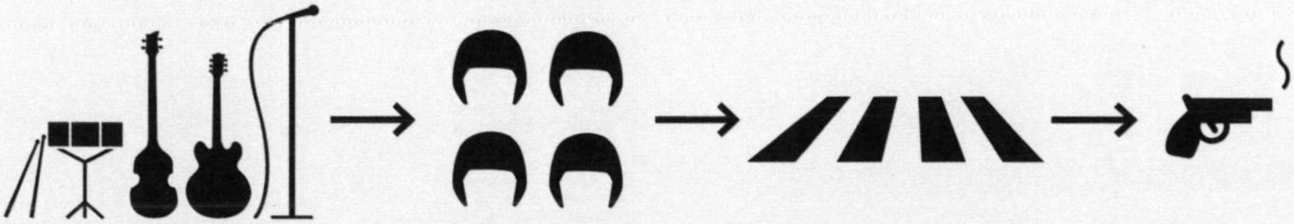

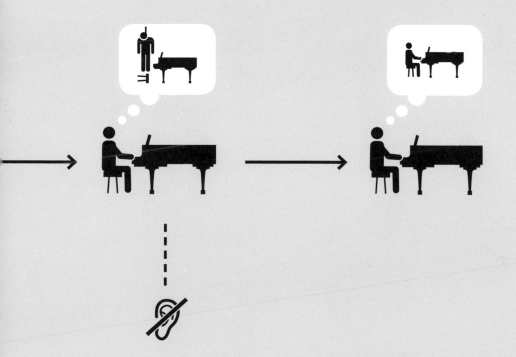

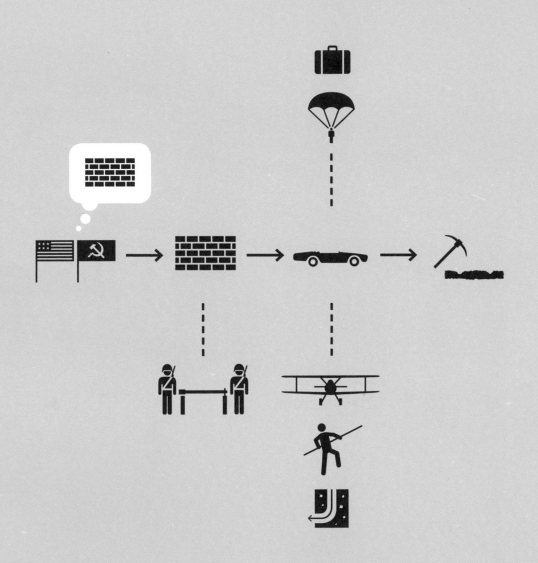

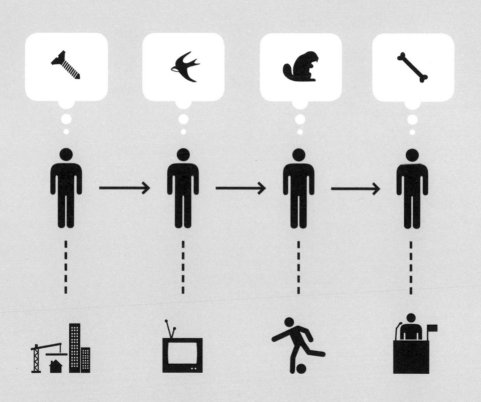

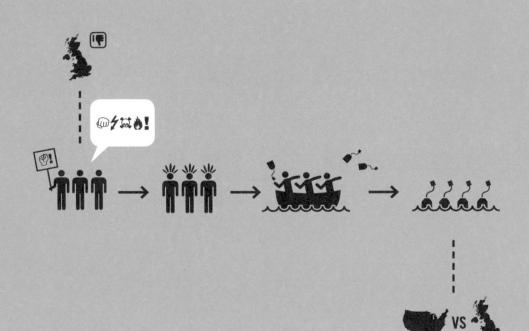

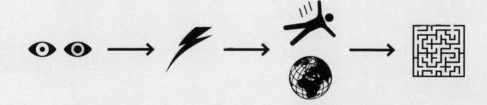

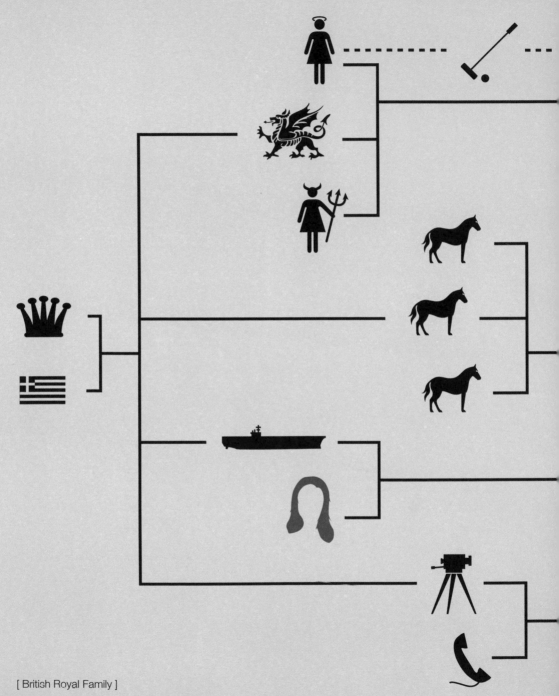

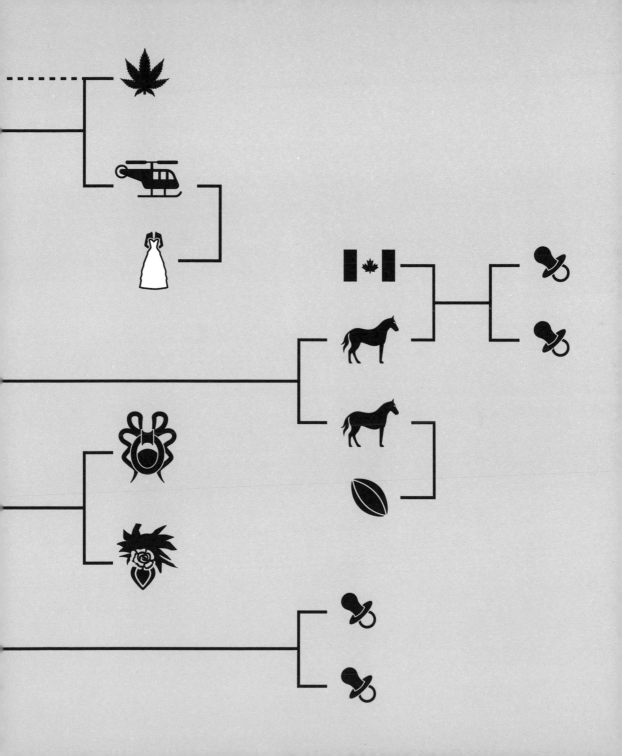

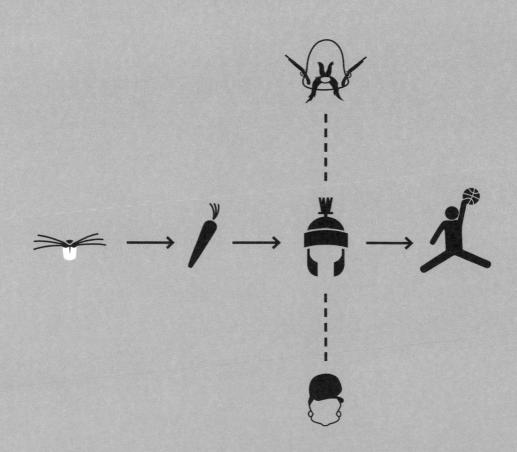

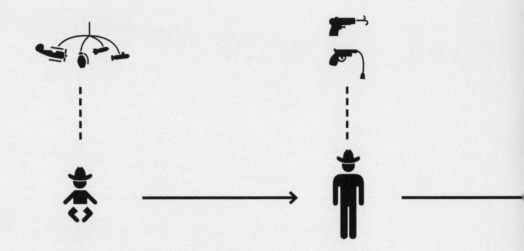

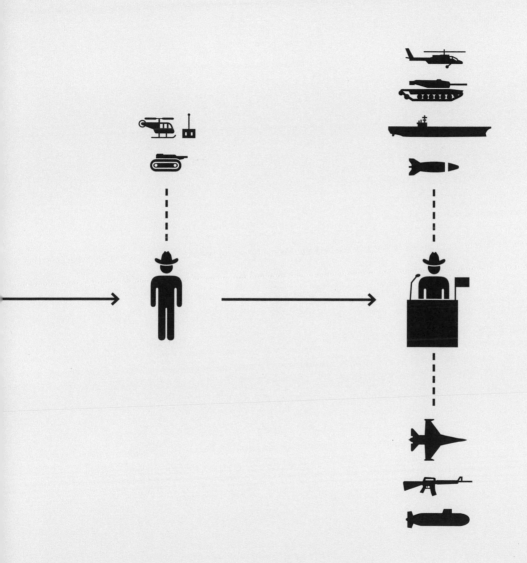

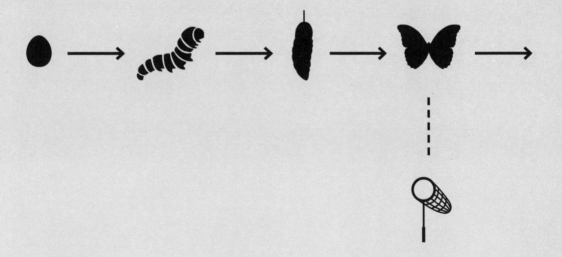

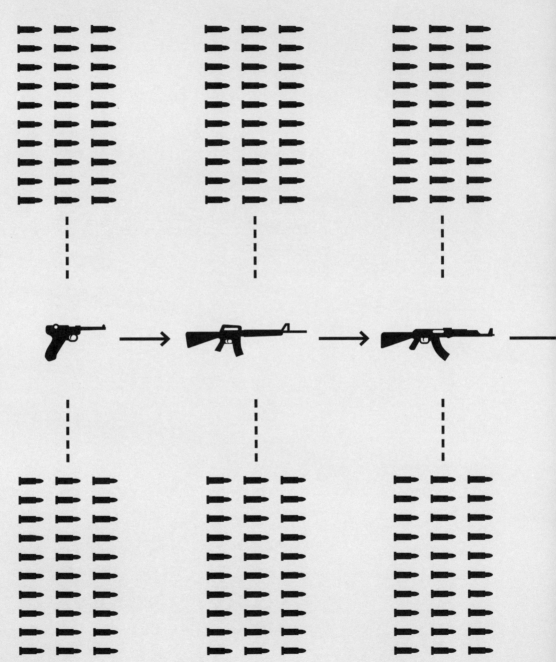

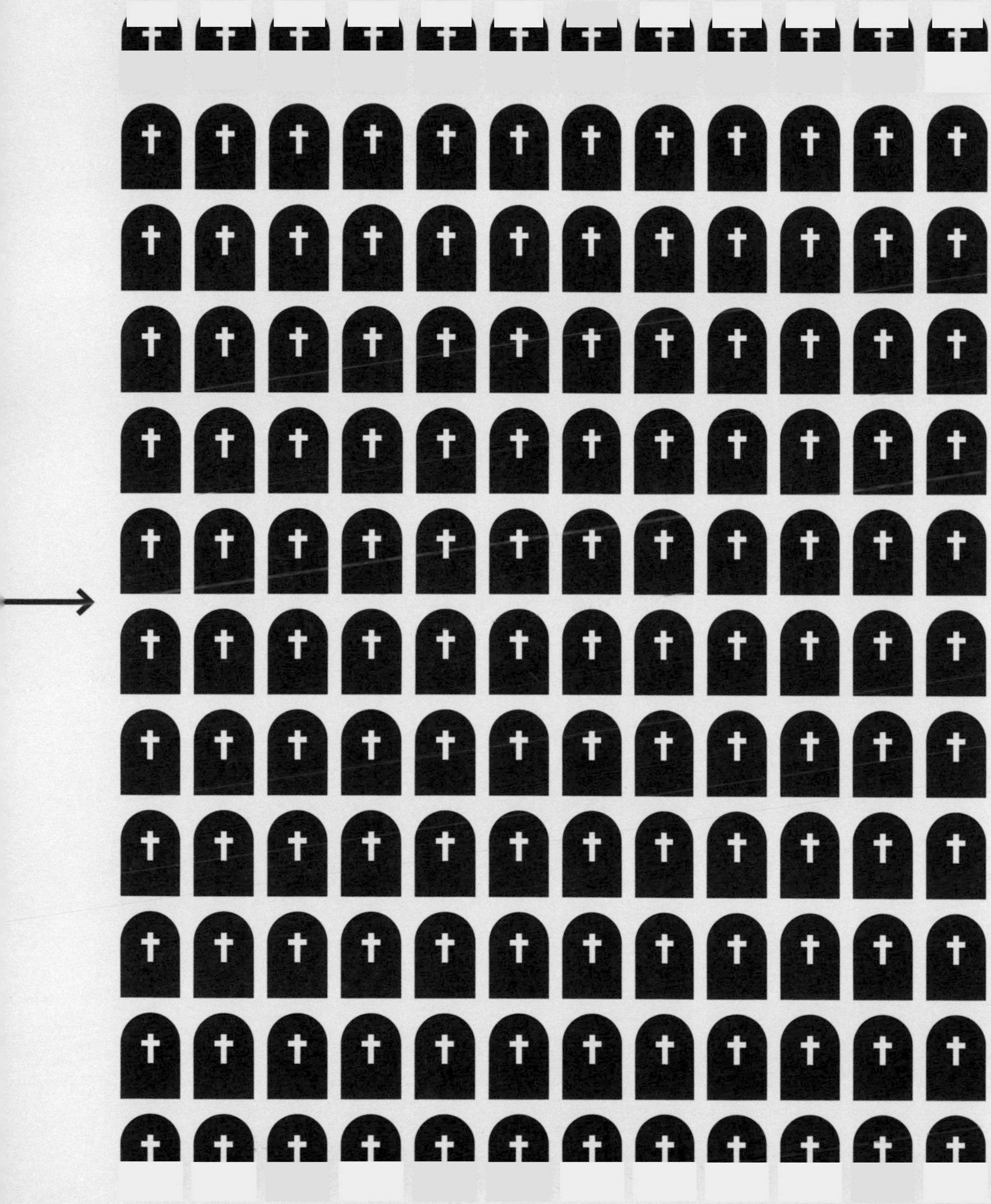

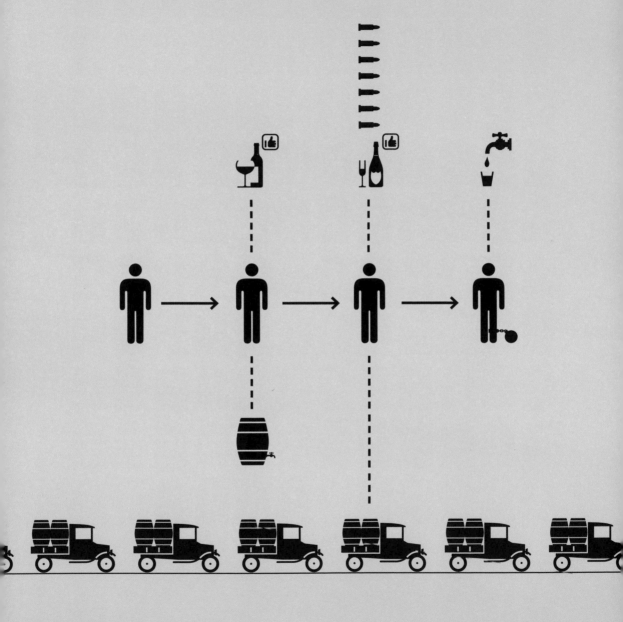

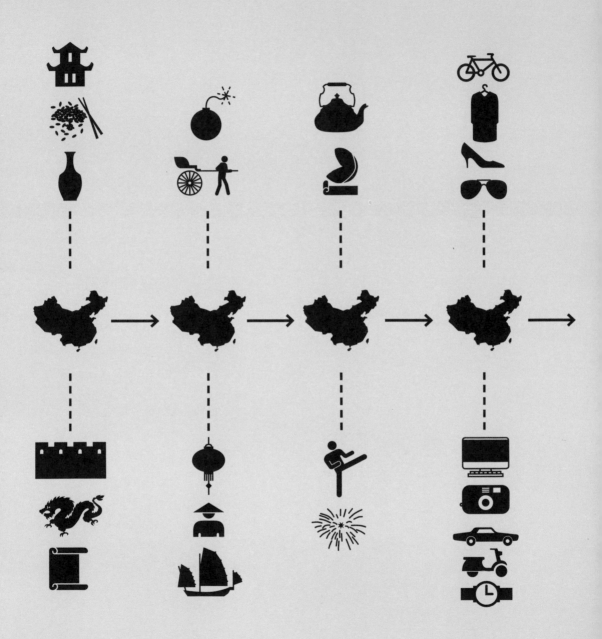

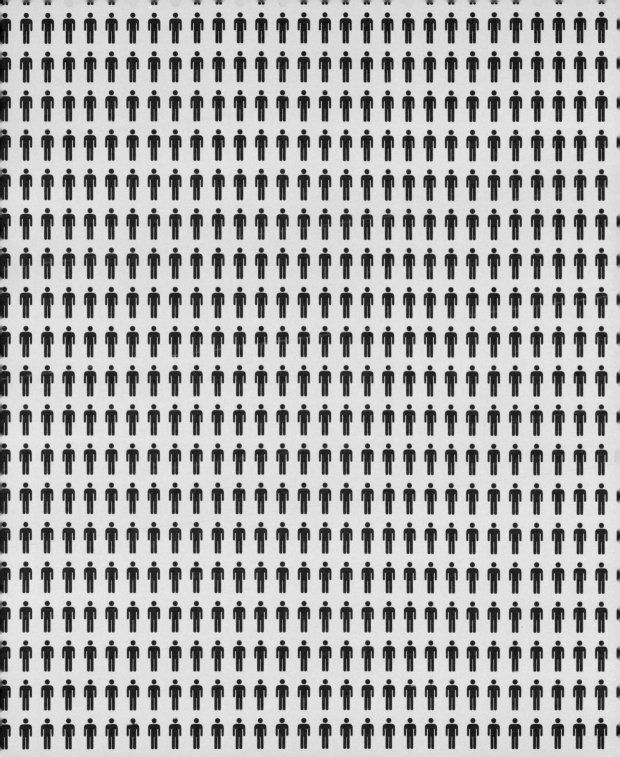

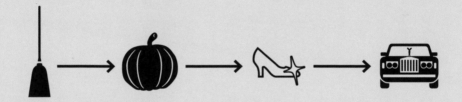

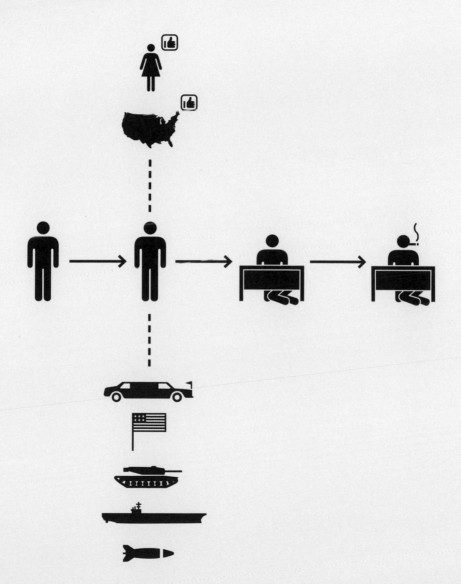

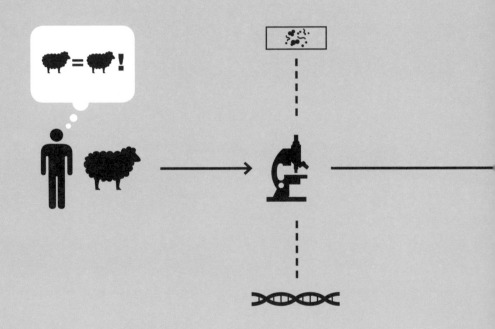

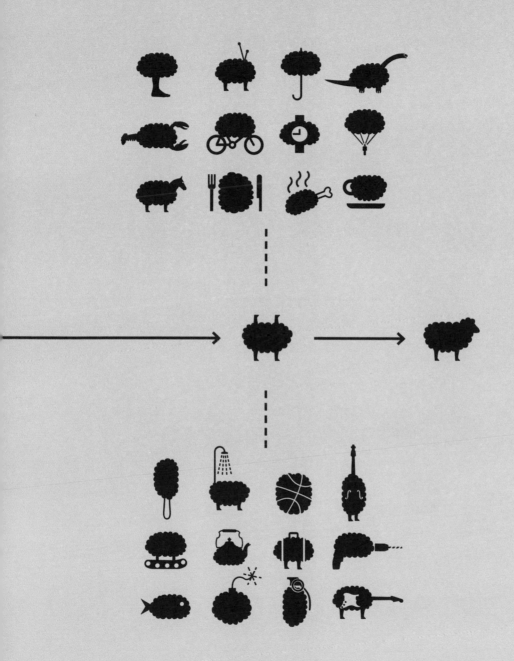

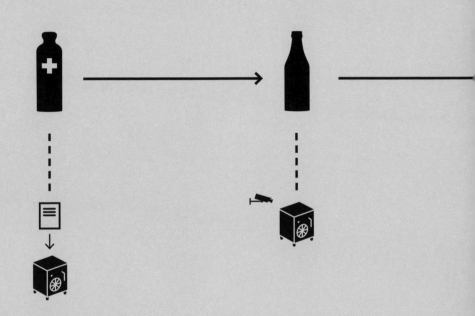

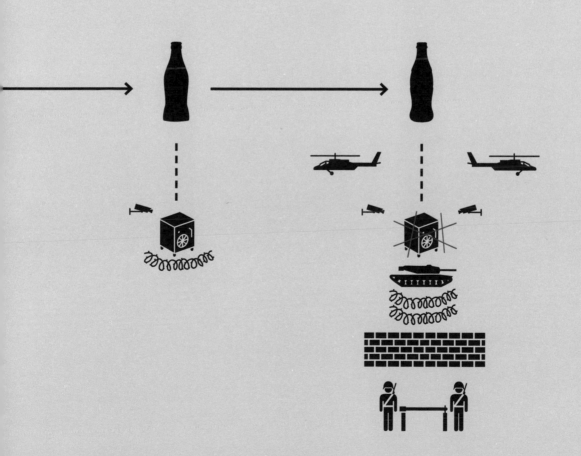

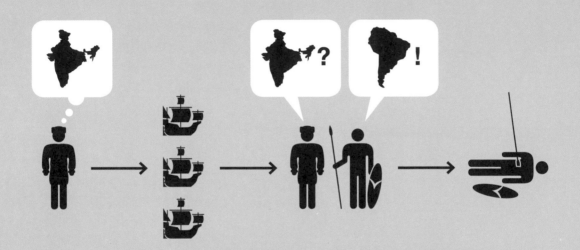

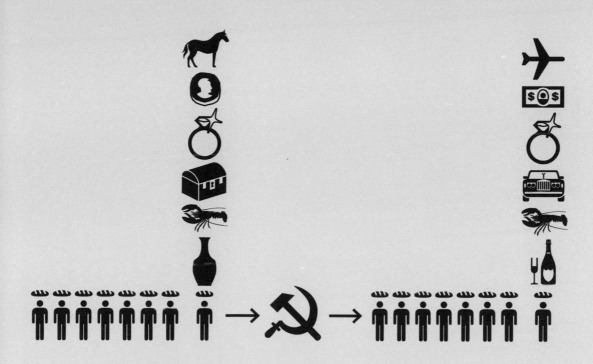

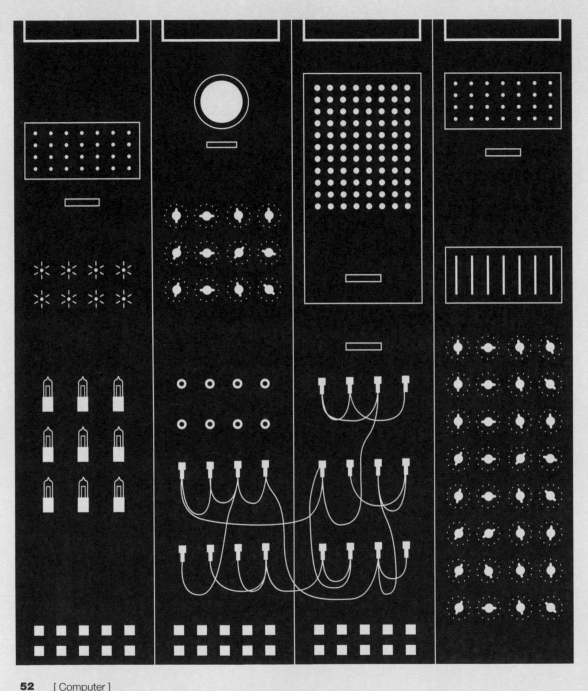

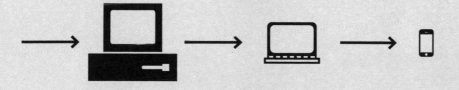

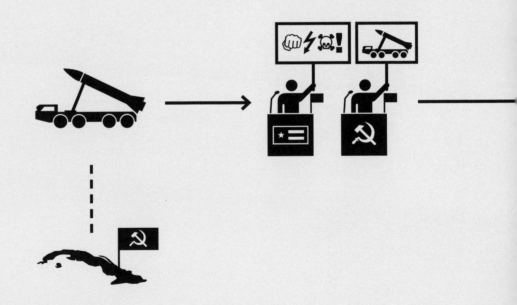

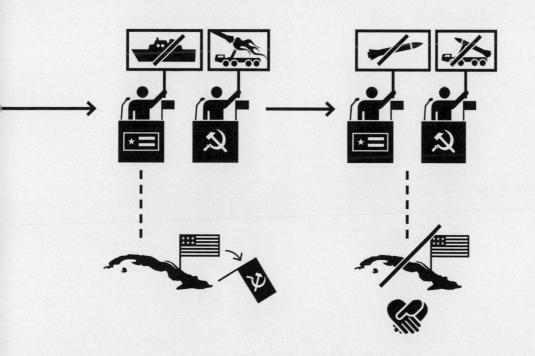

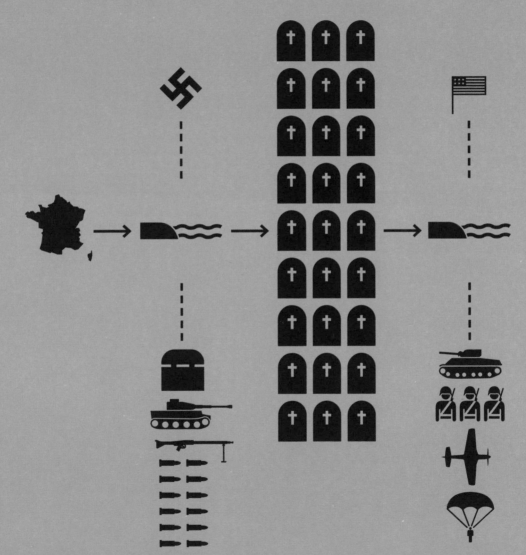

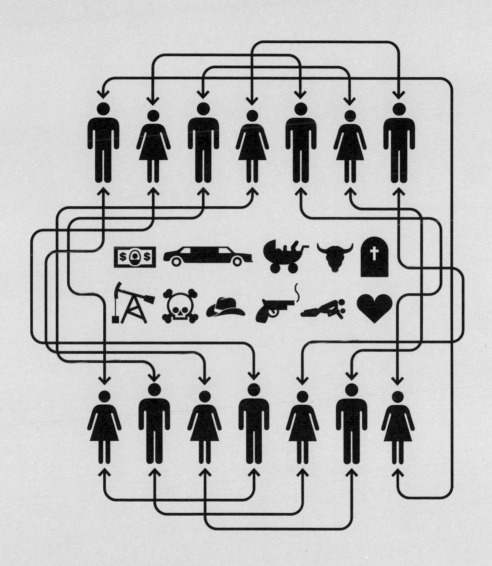

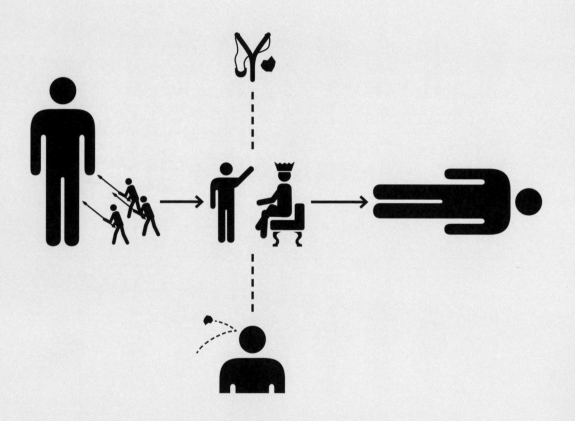

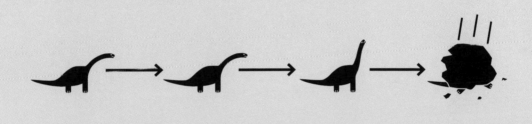

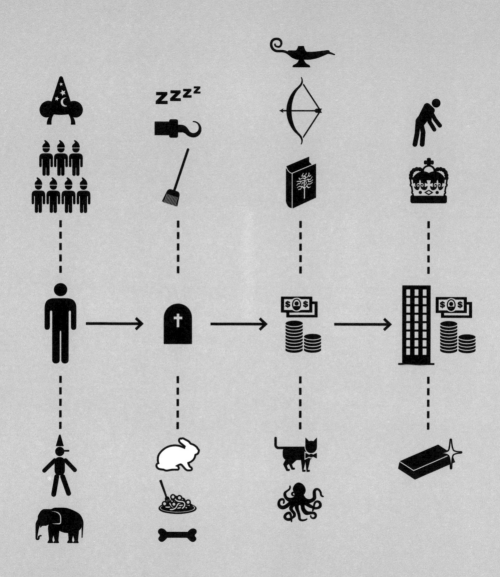

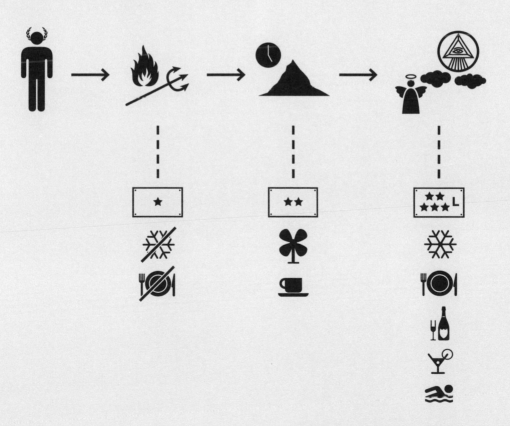

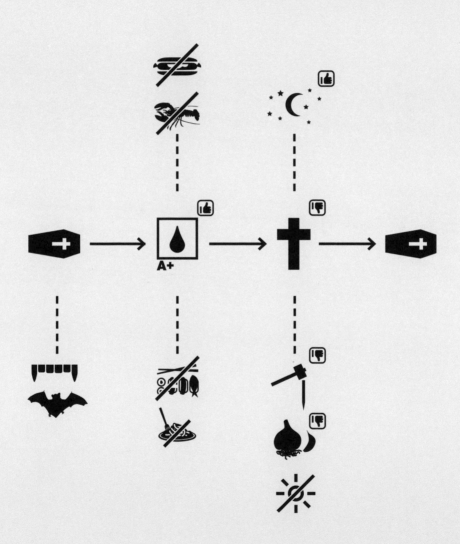

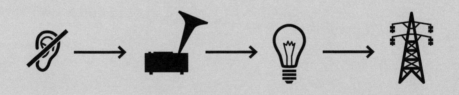

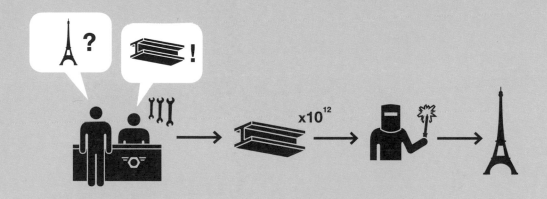

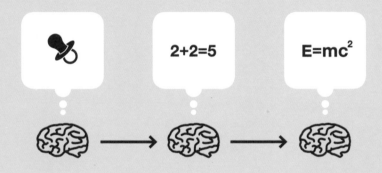

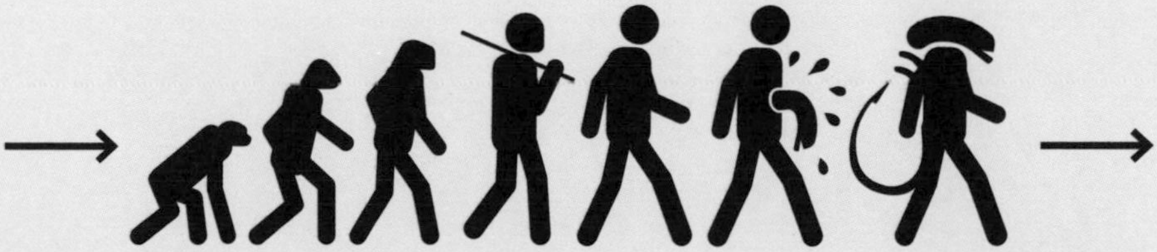

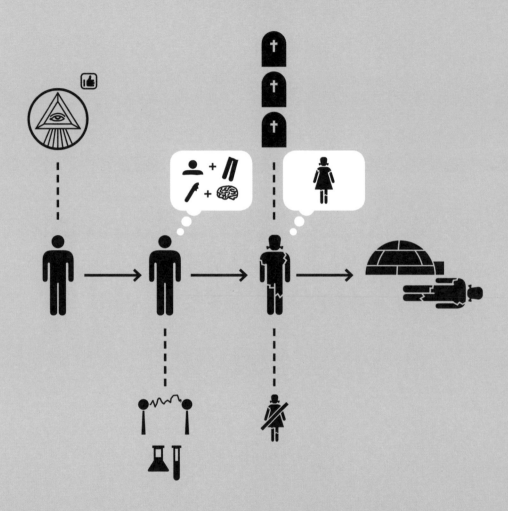

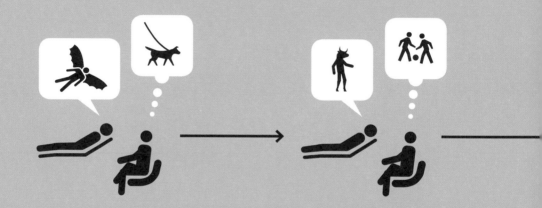

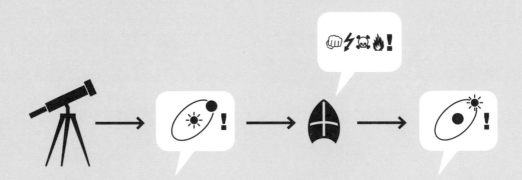

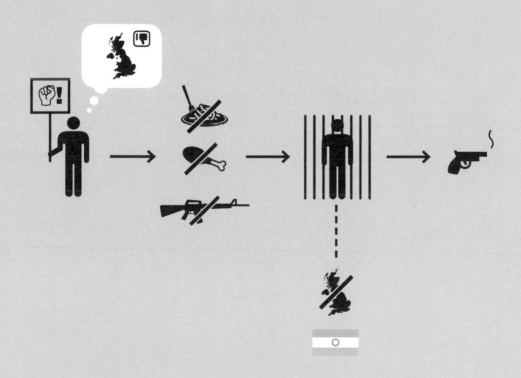

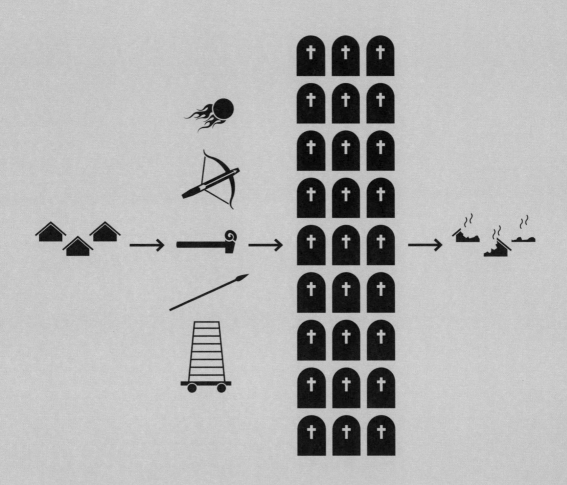

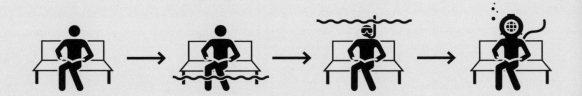

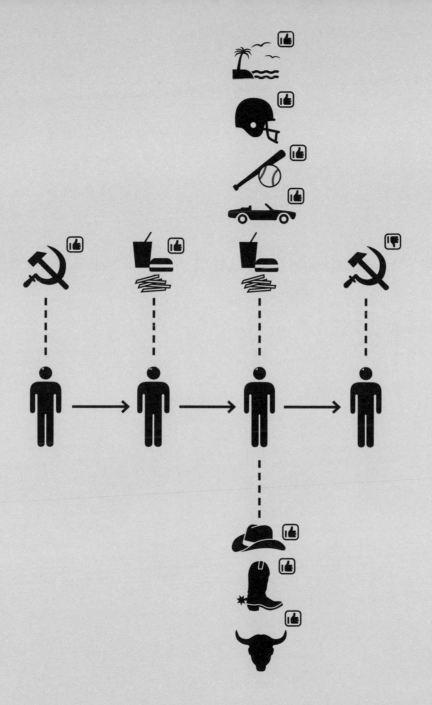

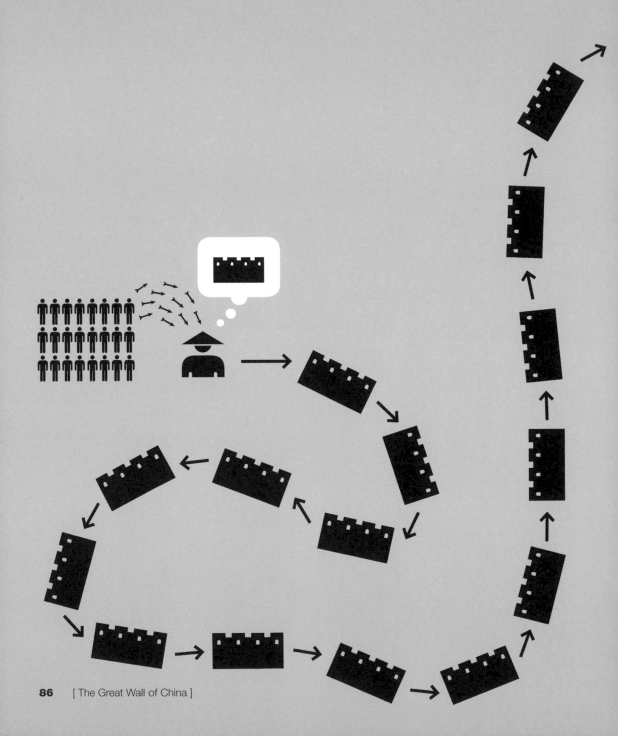

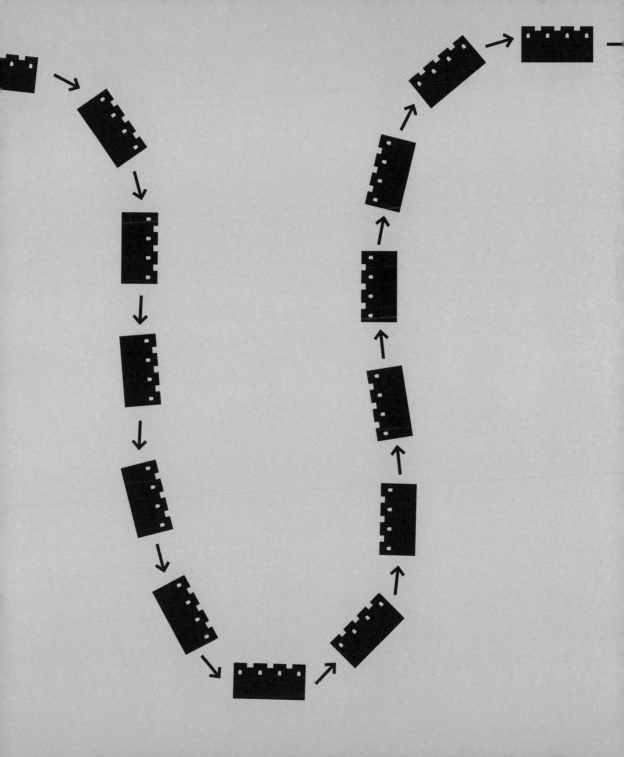

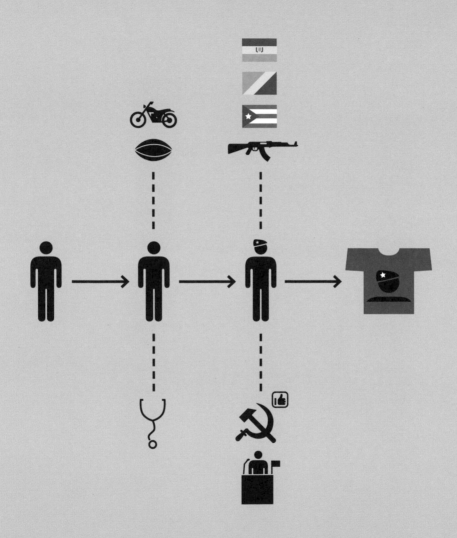

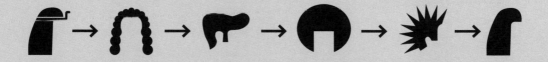

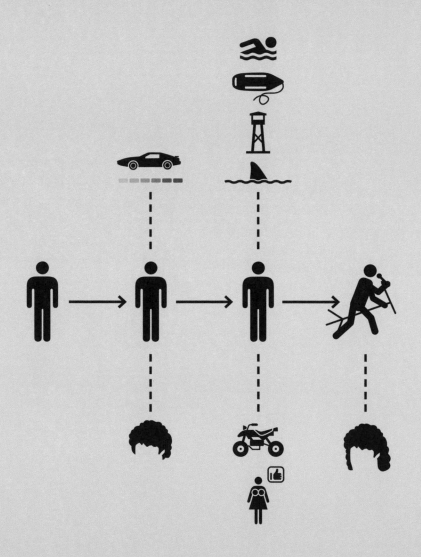

[David Hasselhoff]

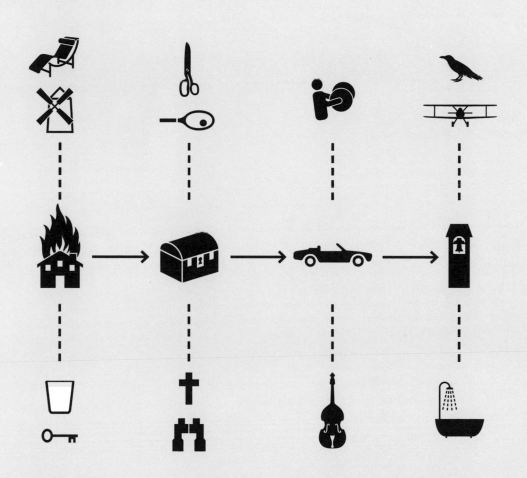

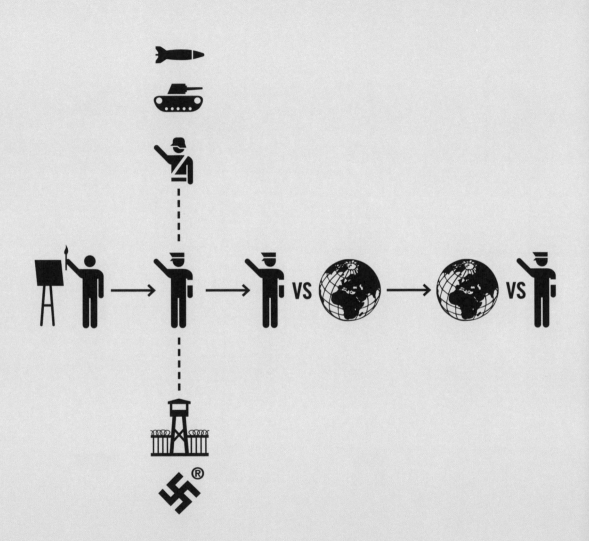

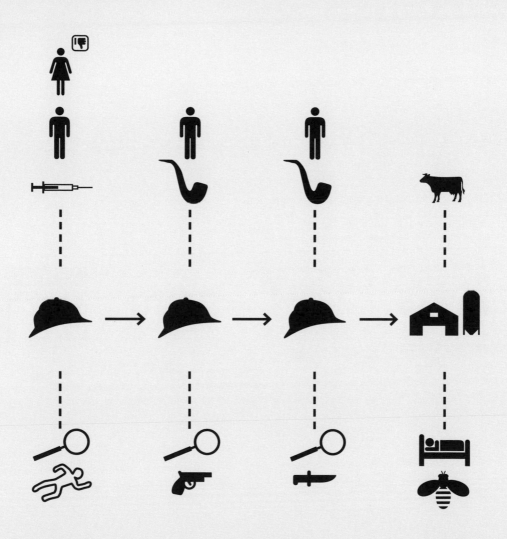

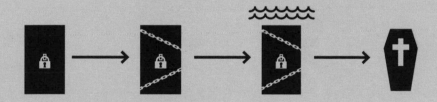

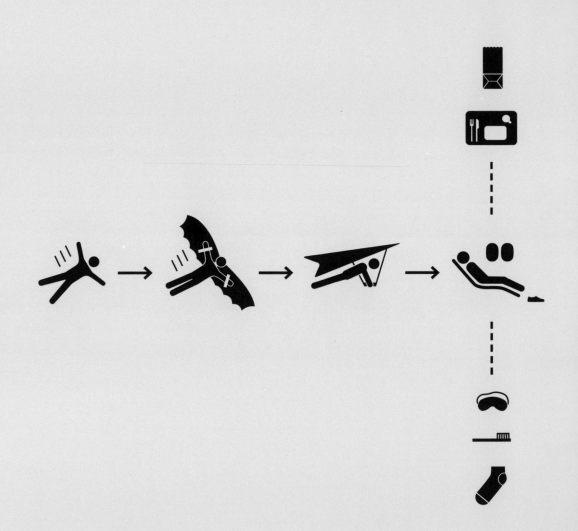

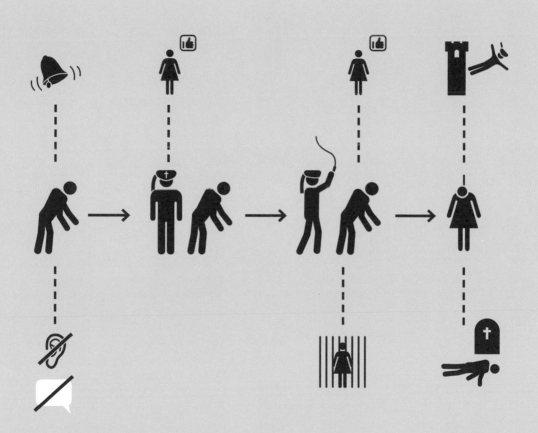

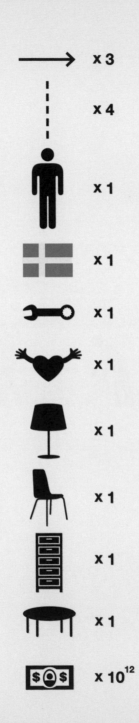

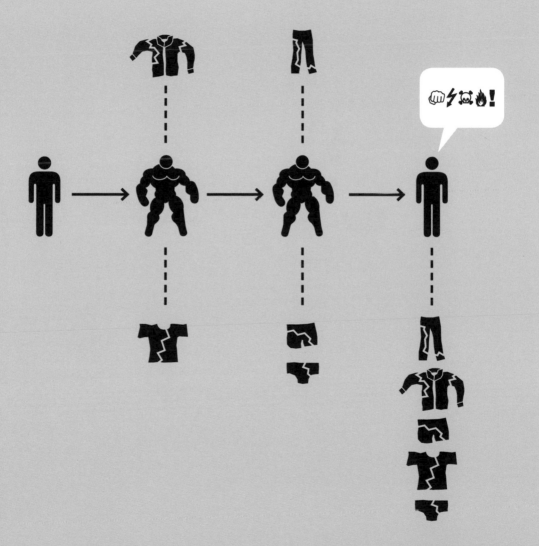

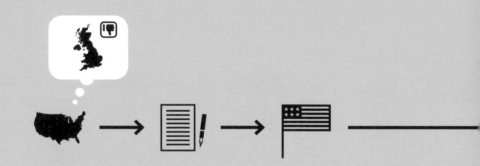

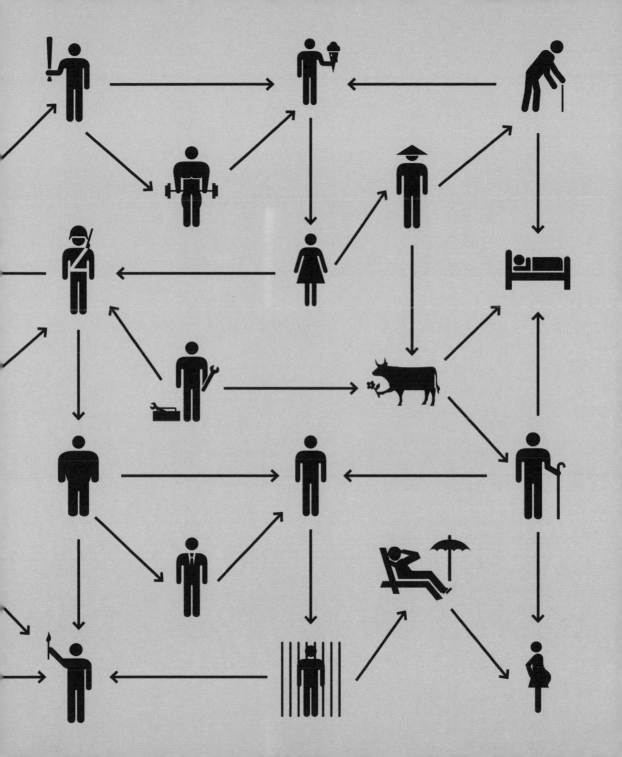

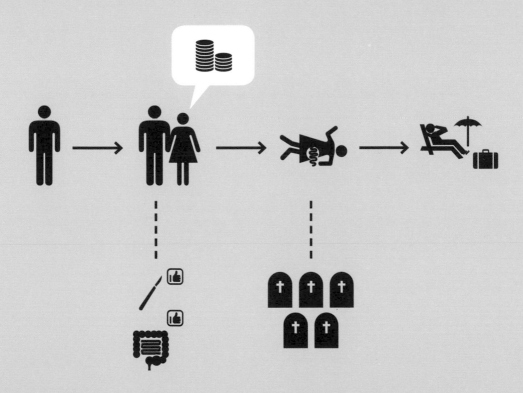

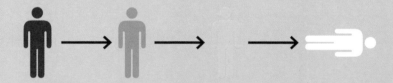

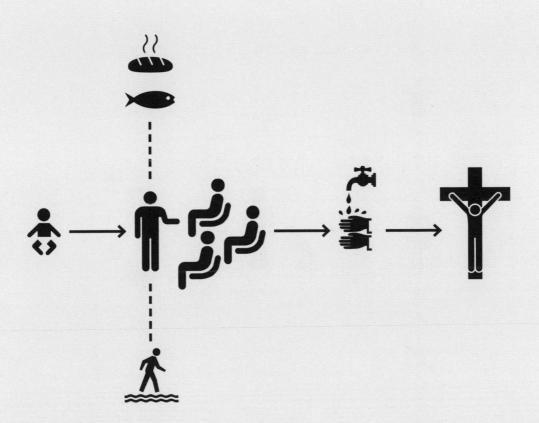

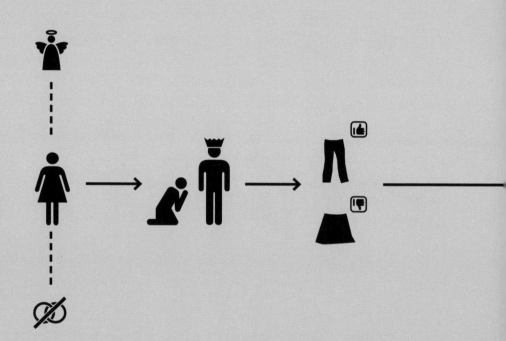

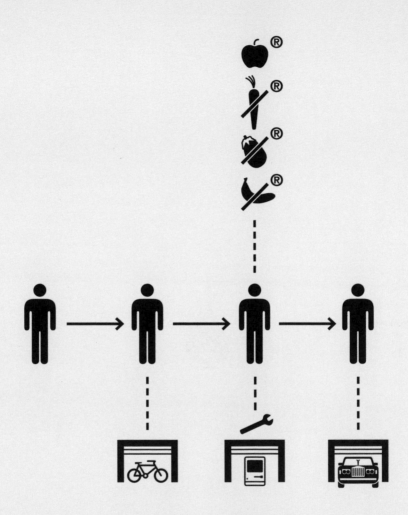

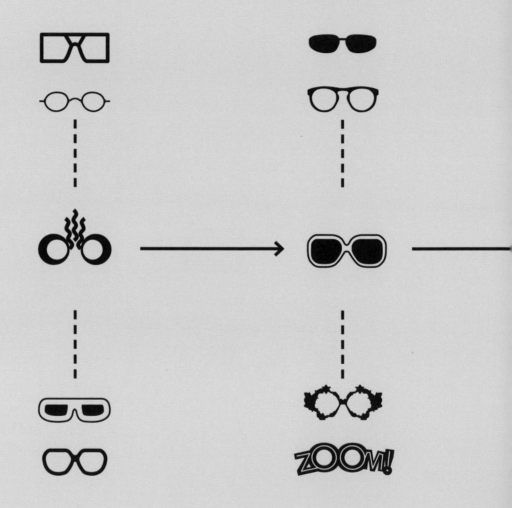

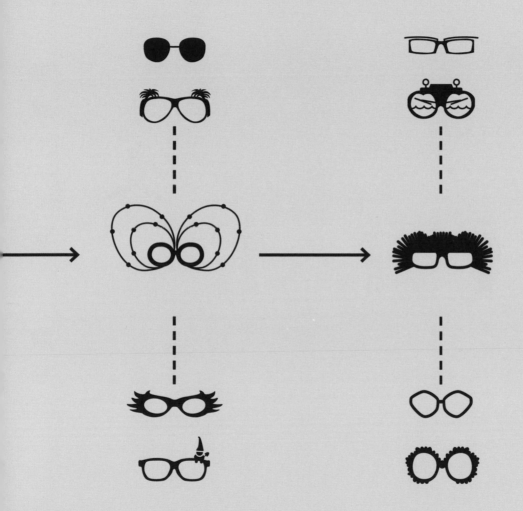

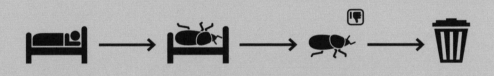

[Kafka's Metamorphosis]

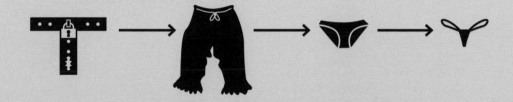

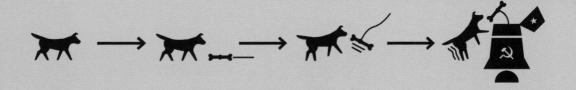

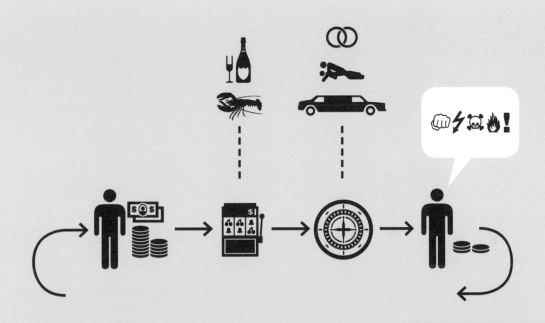

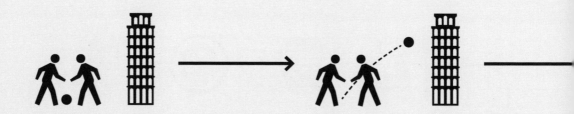

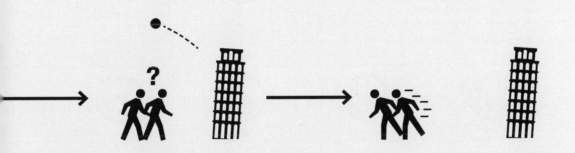

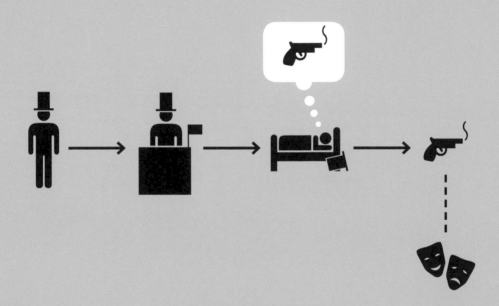

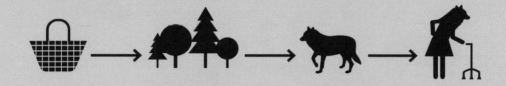

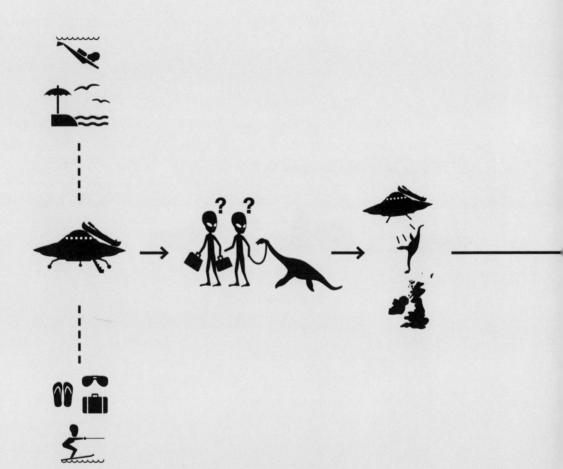

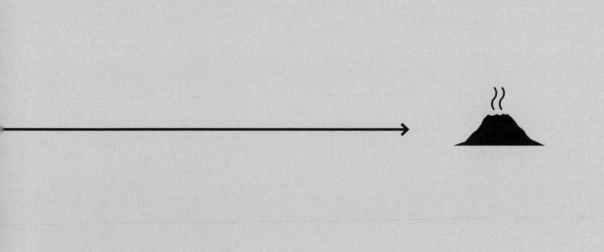

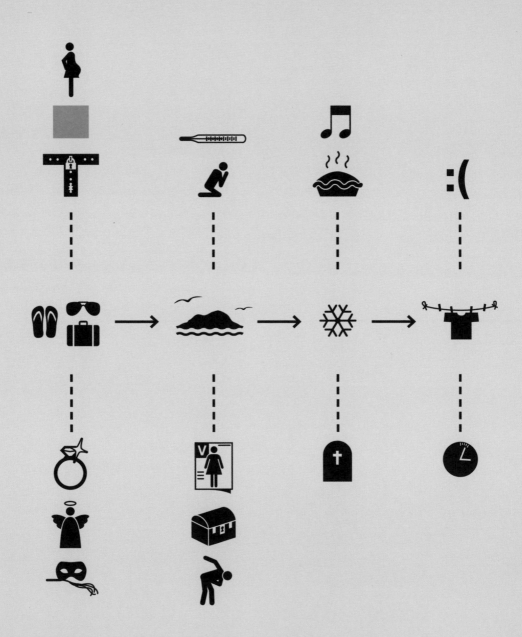

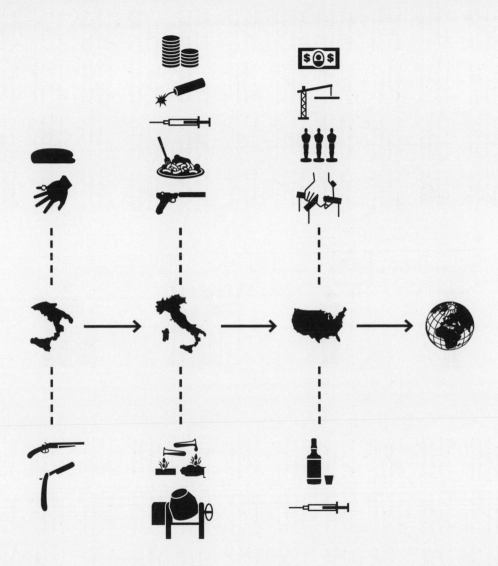

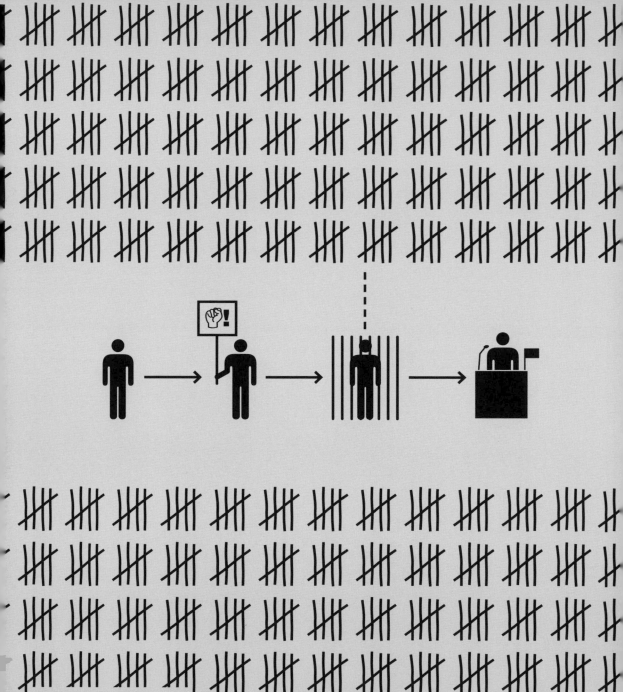

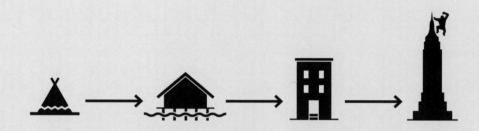

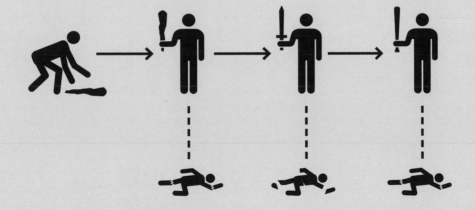

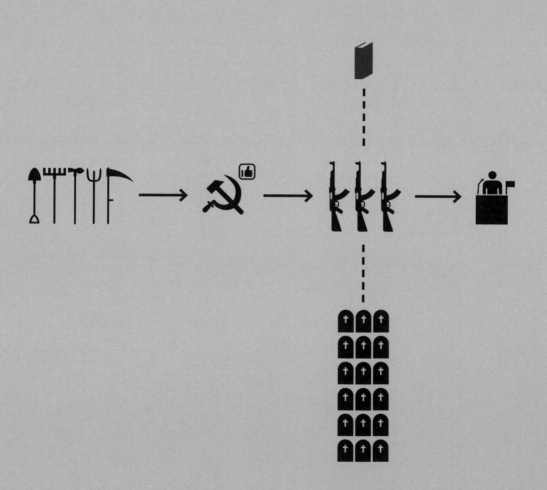

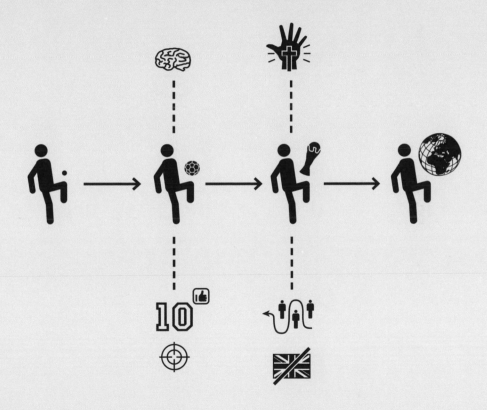

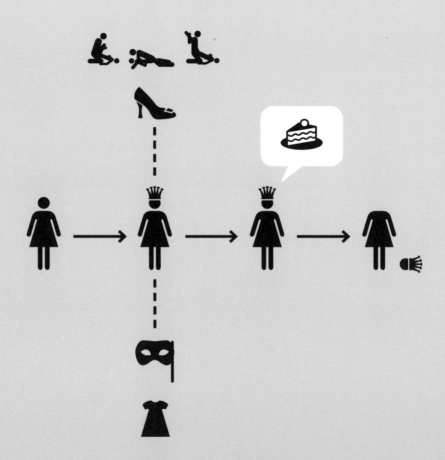

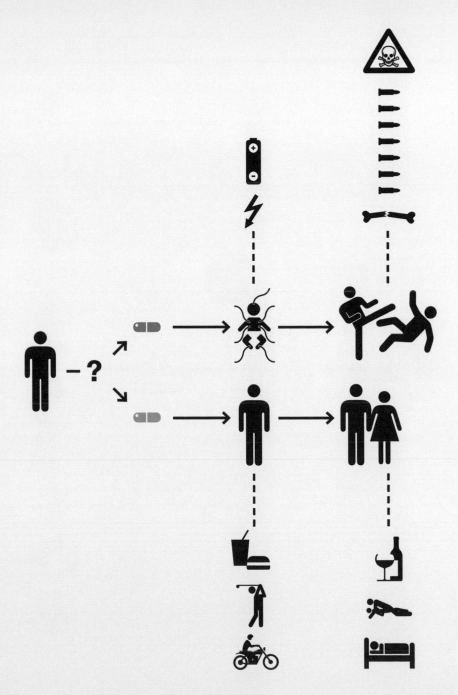

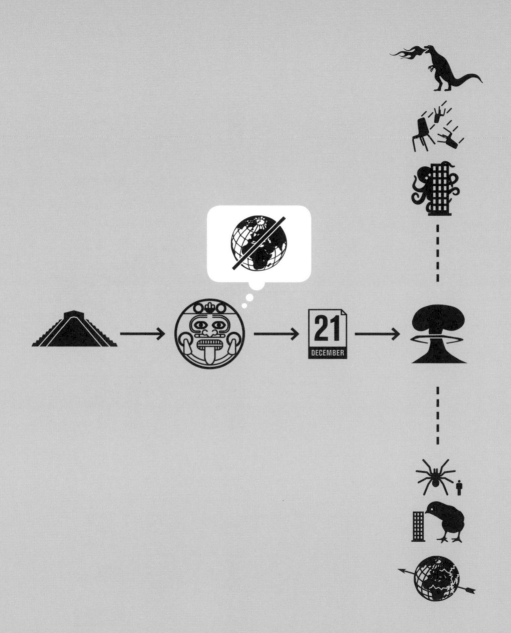

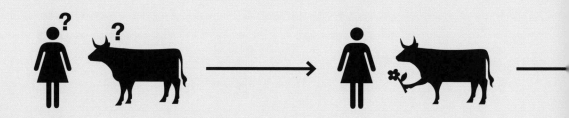

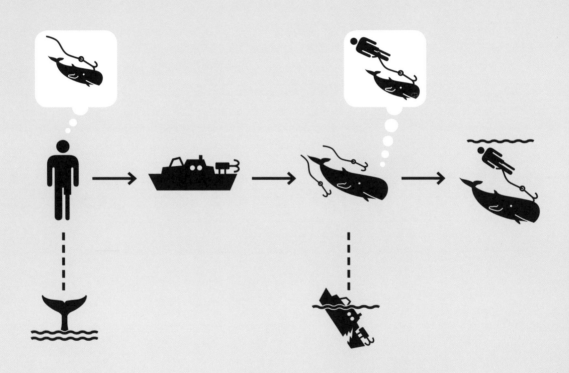

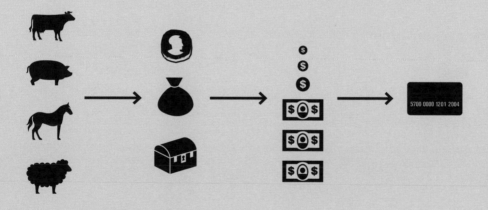

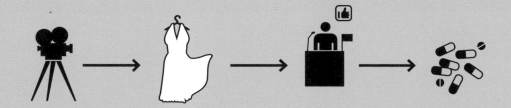

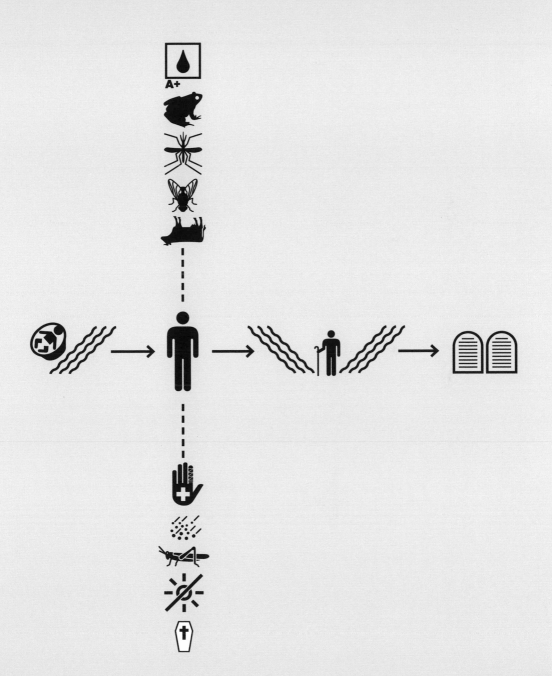

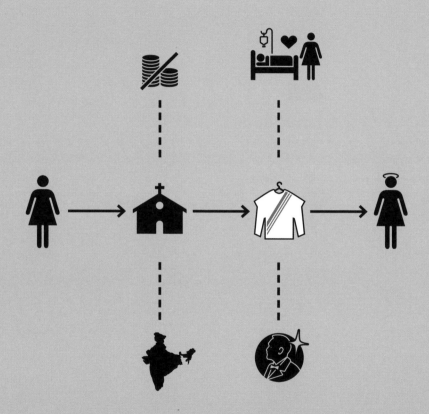

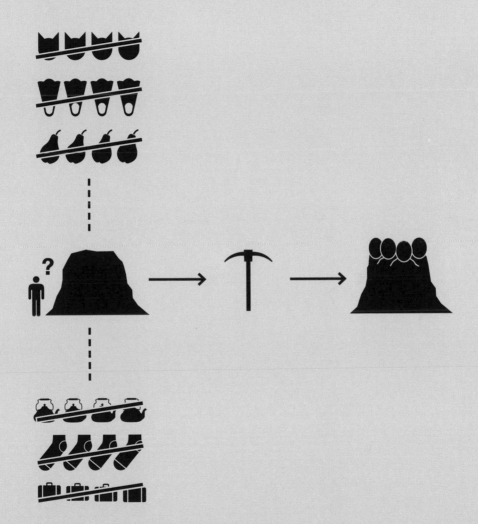

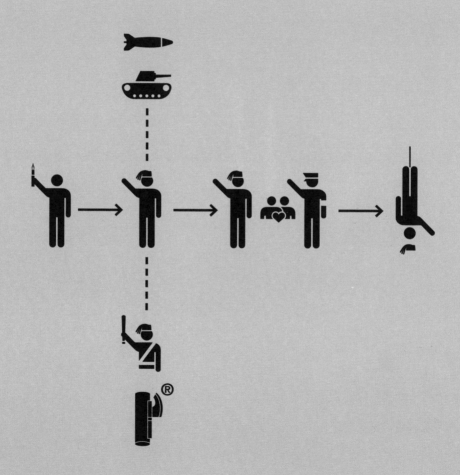

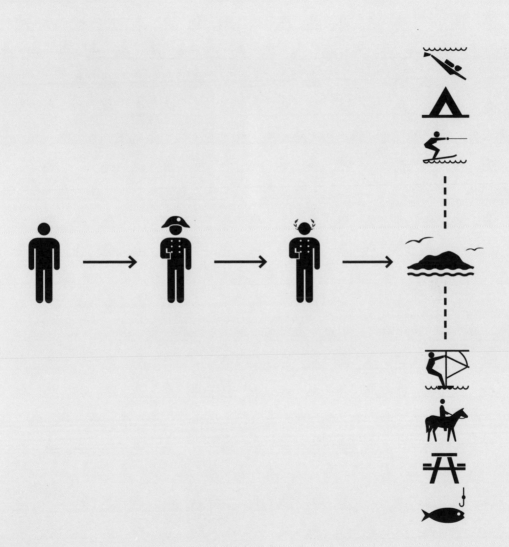

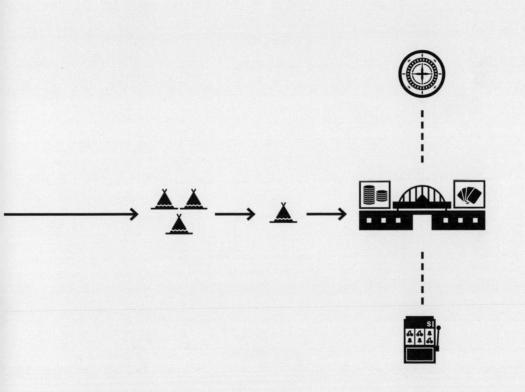

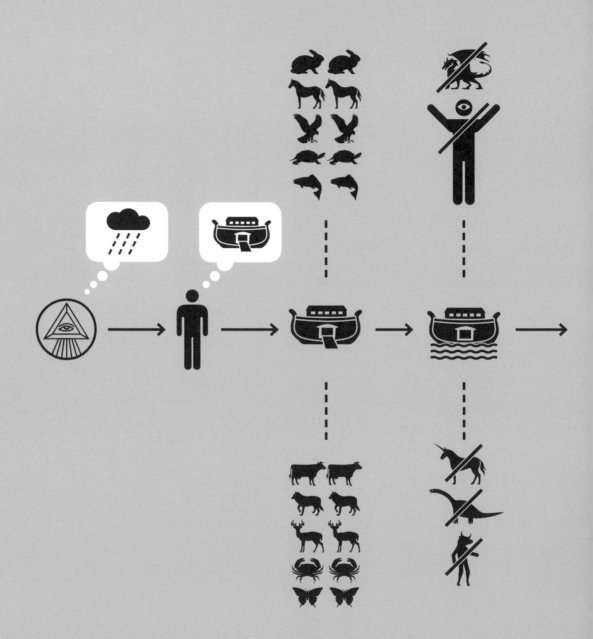

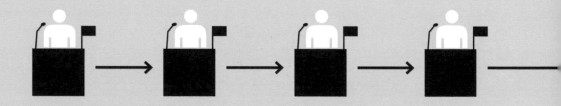

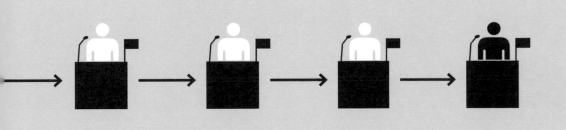

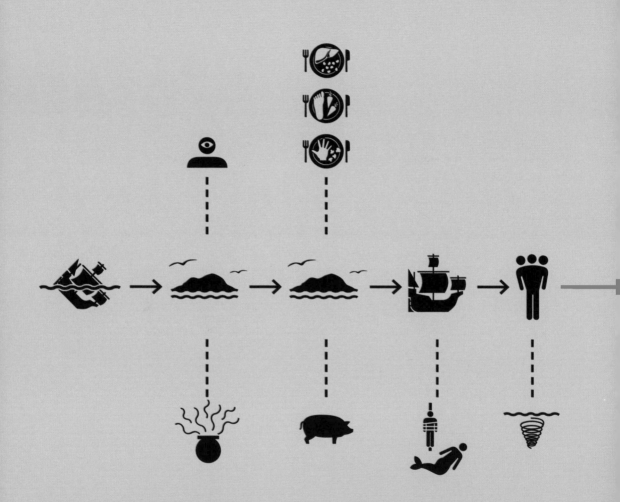

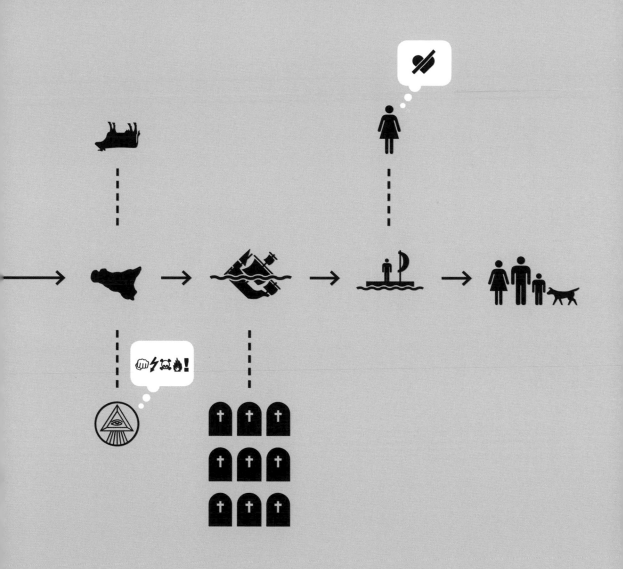

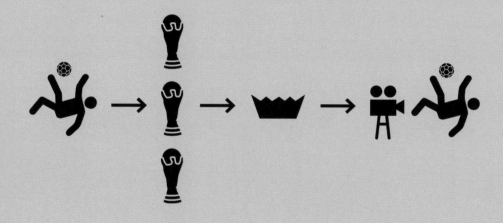

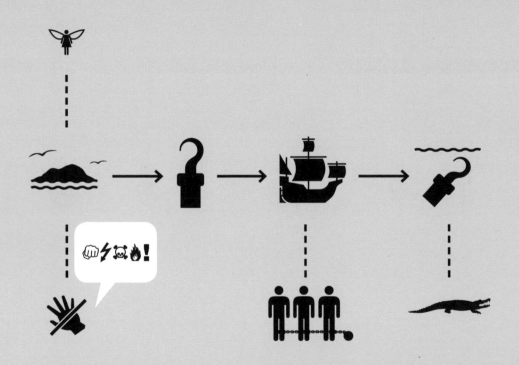

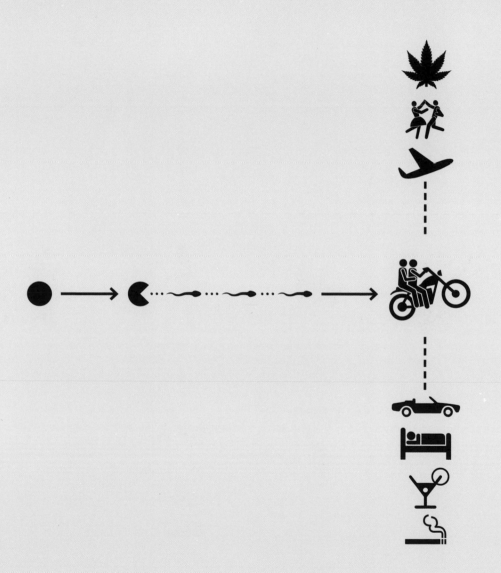

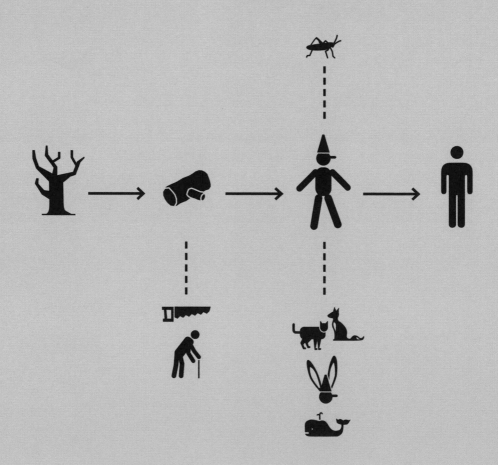

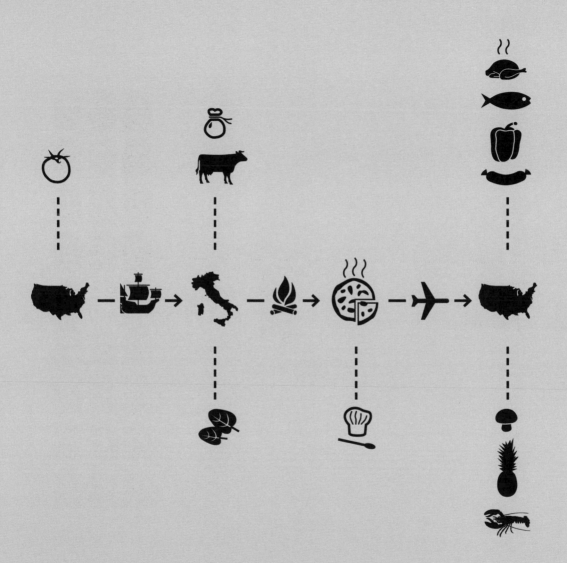

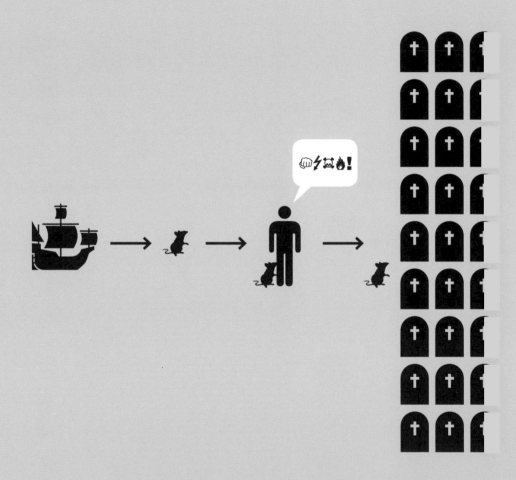

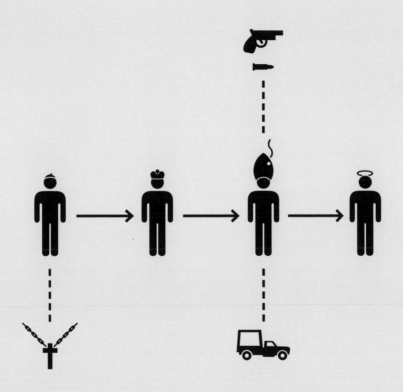

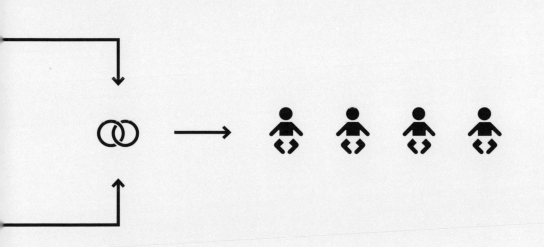

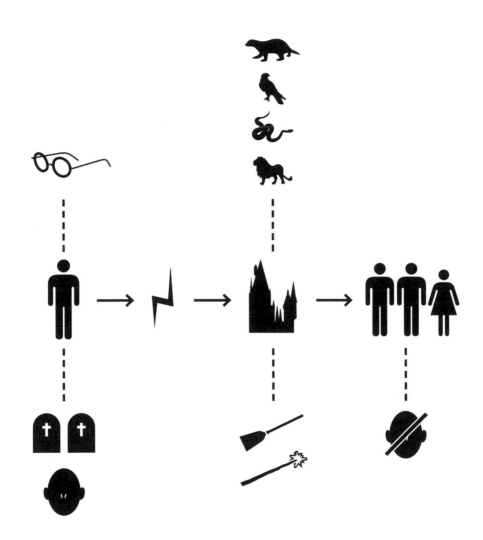

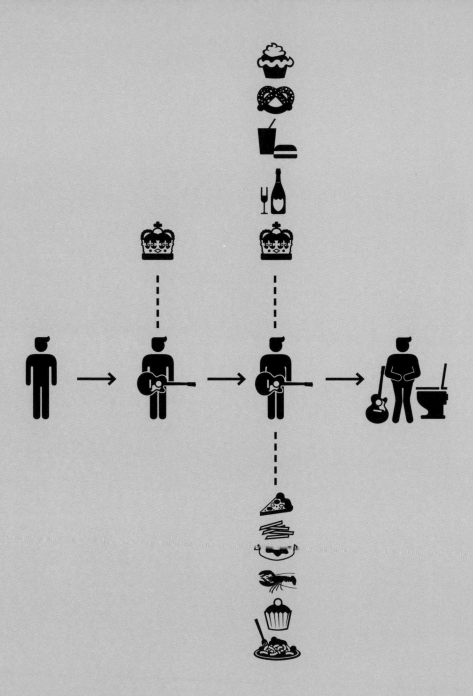

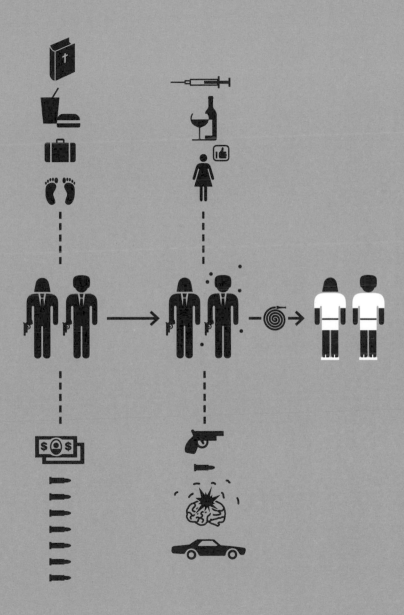

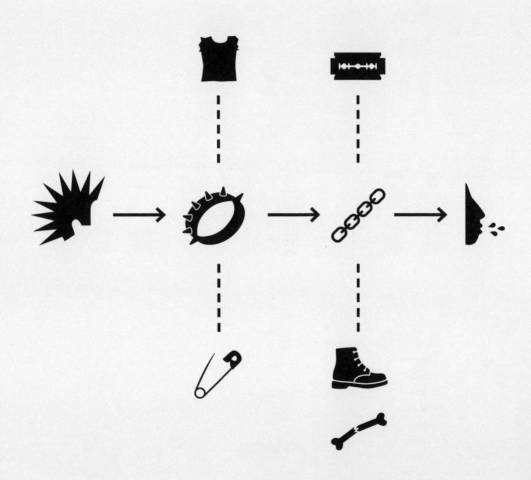

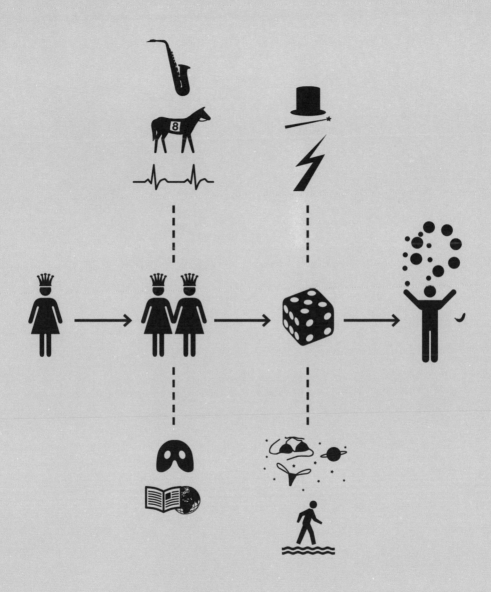

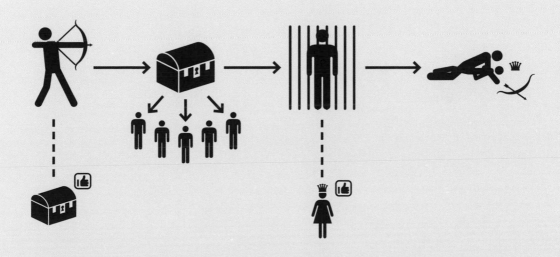

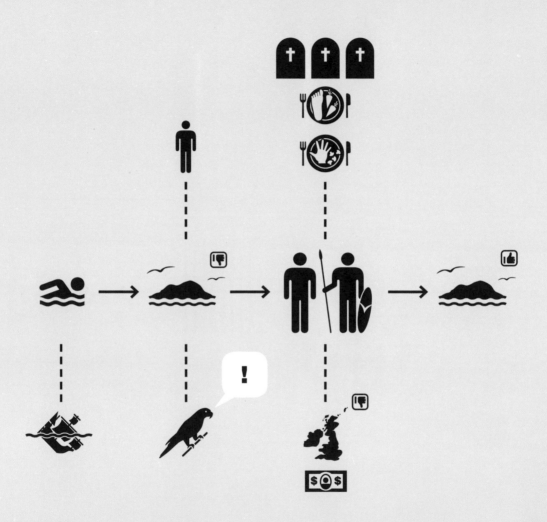

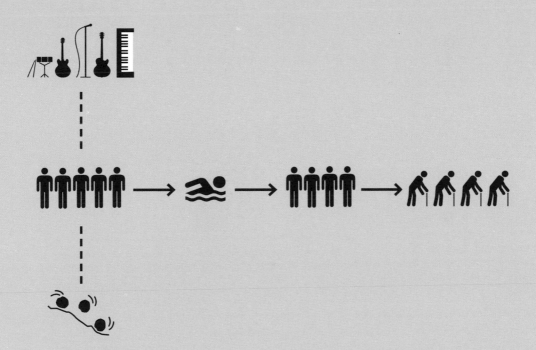

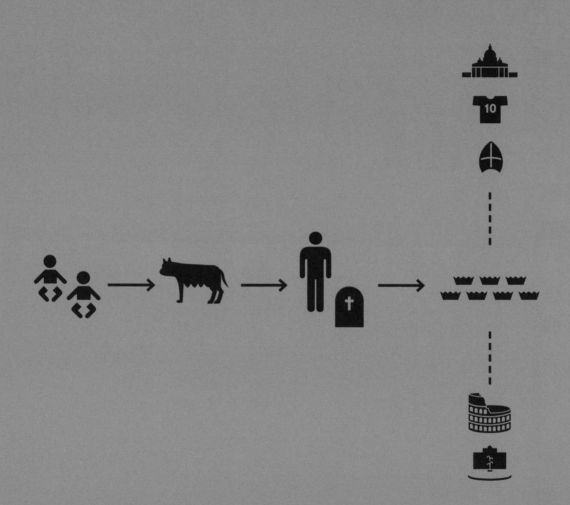

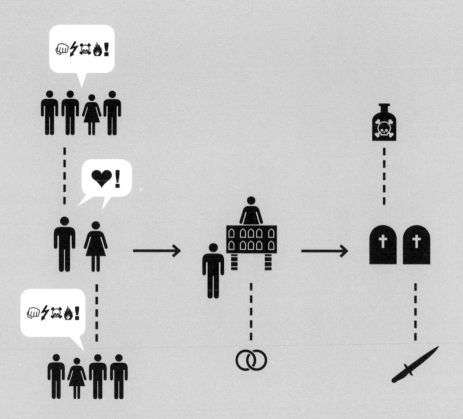

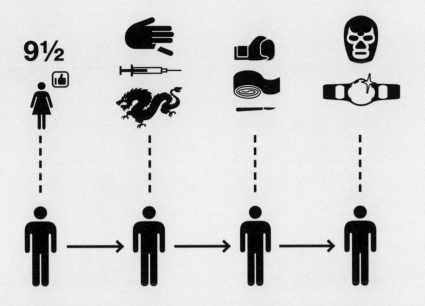

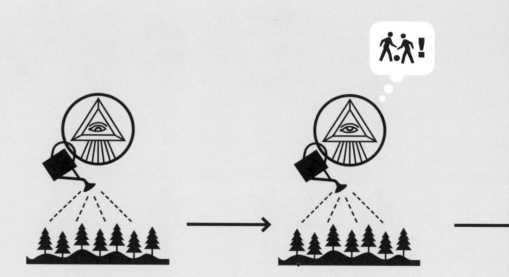

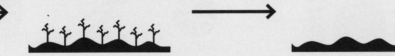

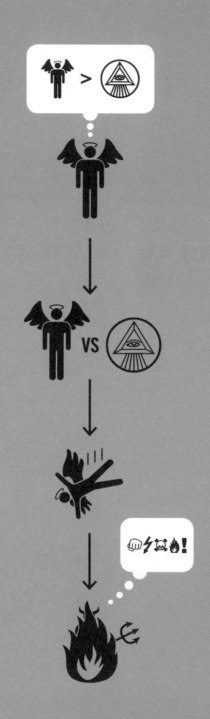

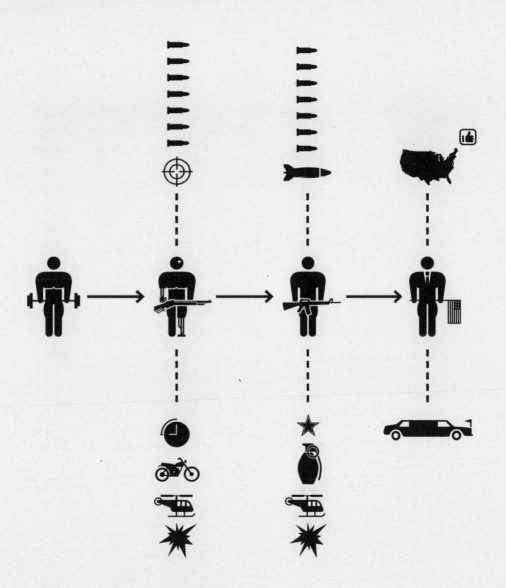

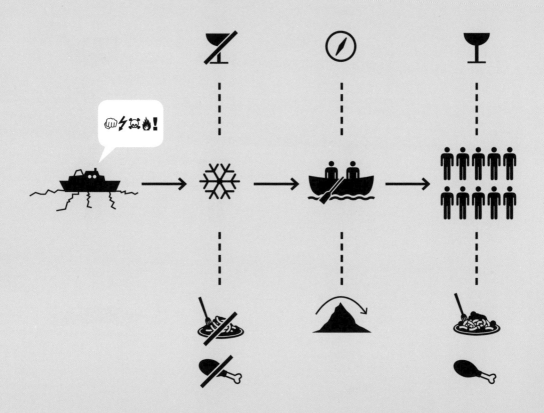

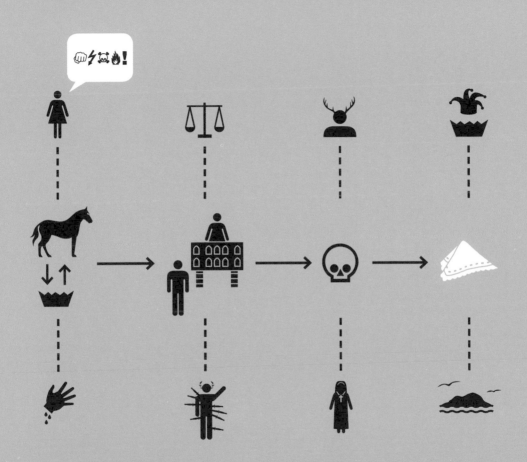

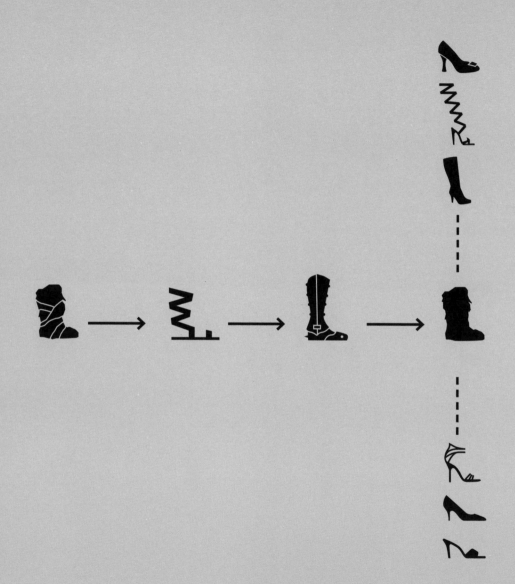

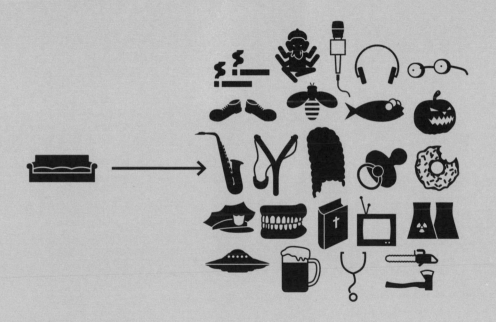

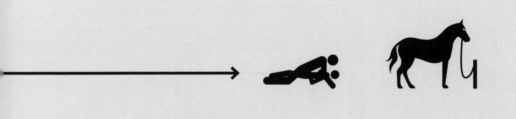

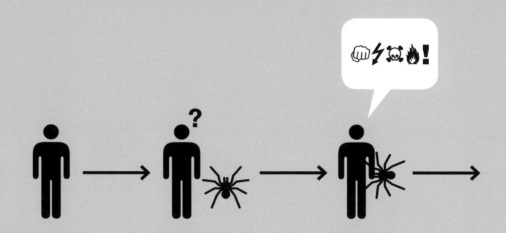

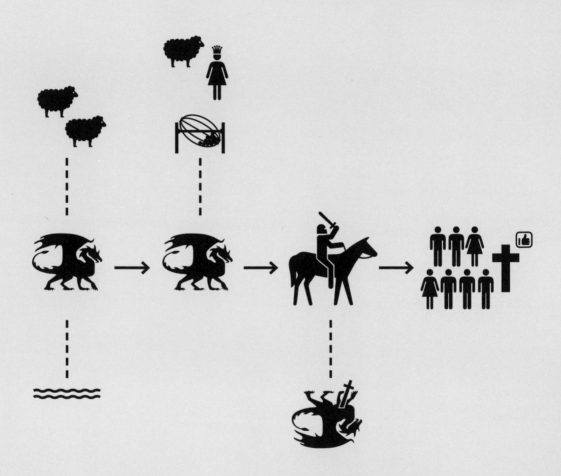

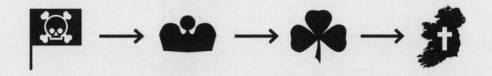

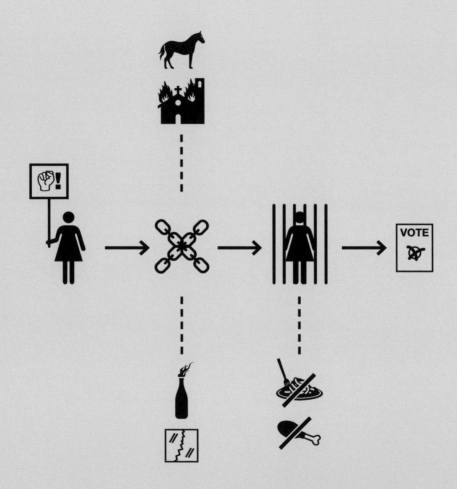

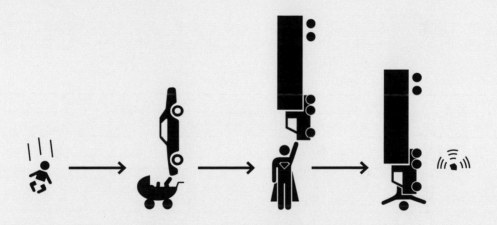

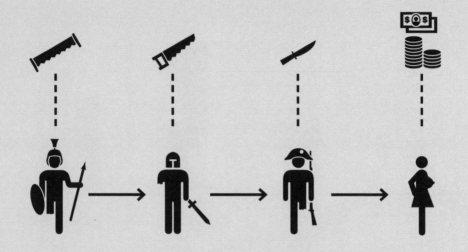

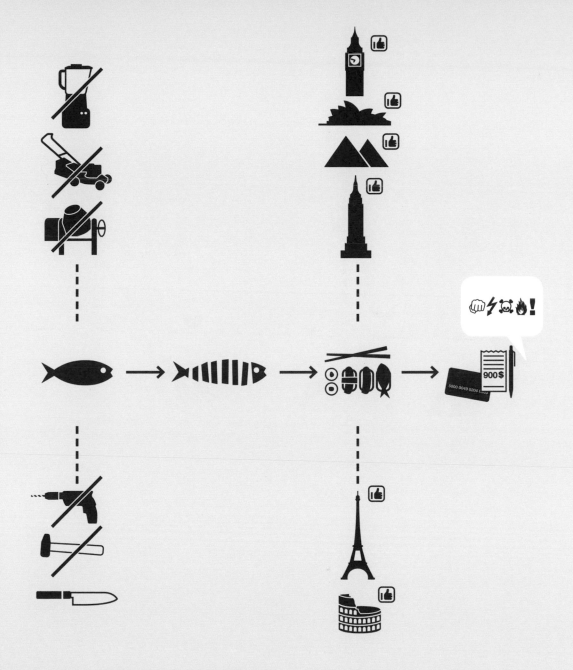

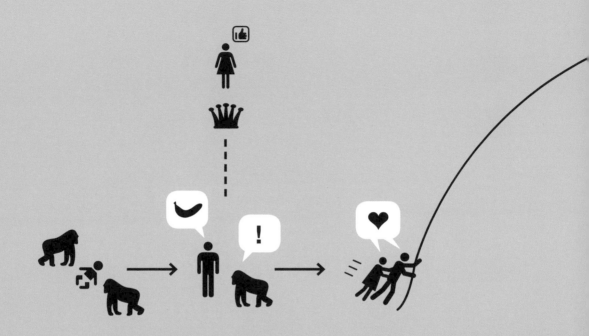

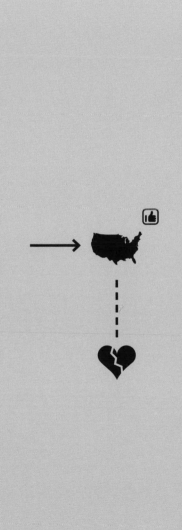

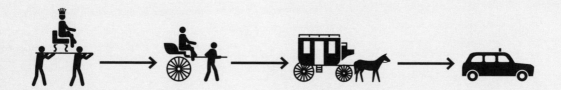

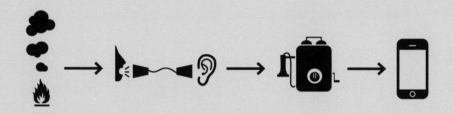

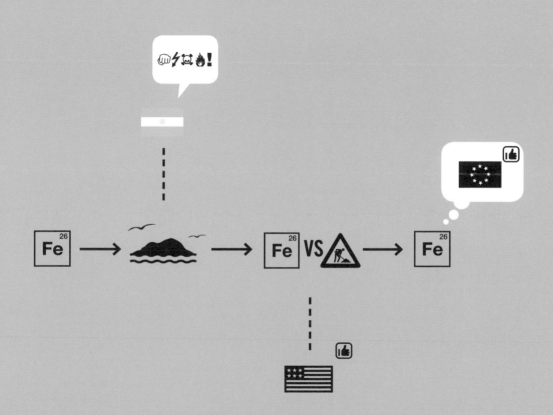

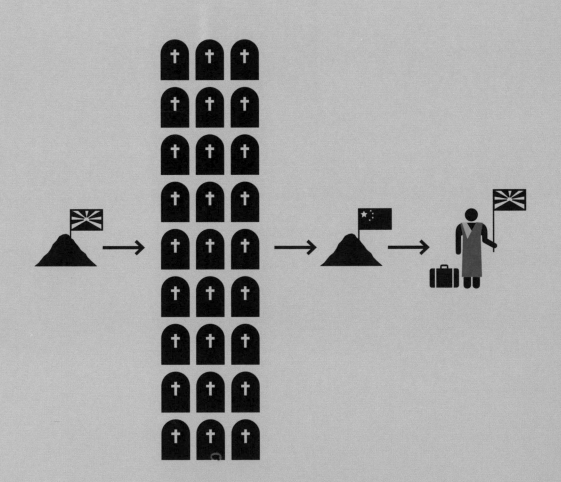

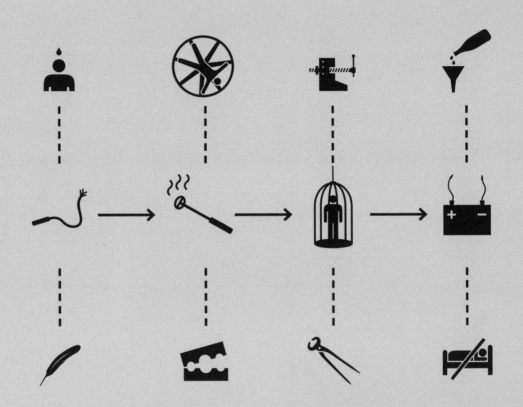

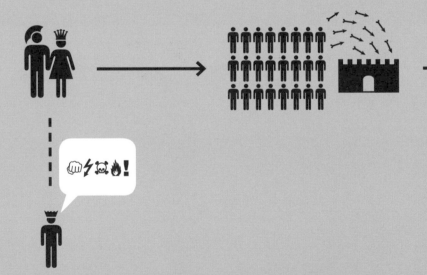

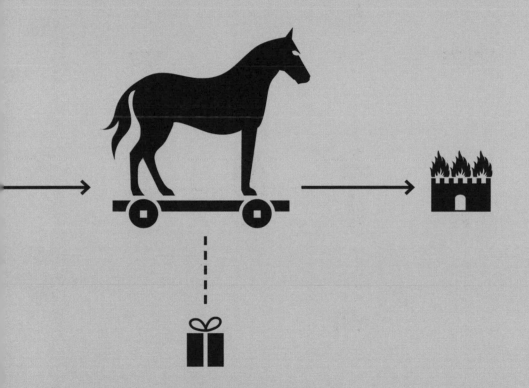

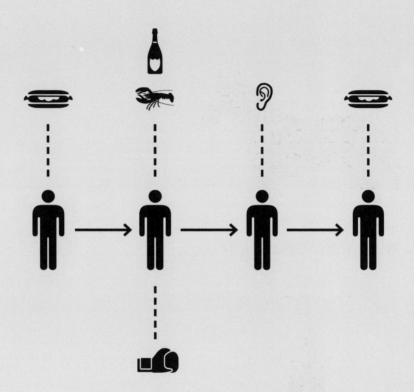

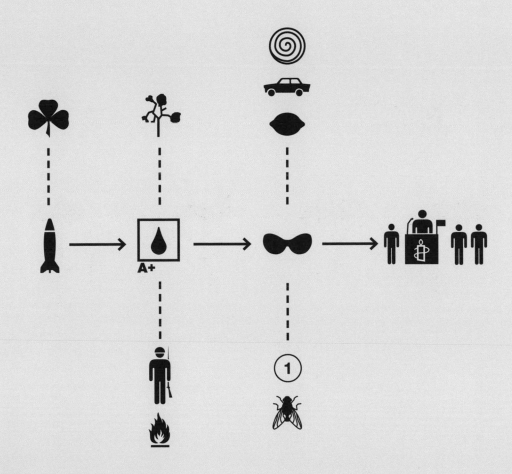

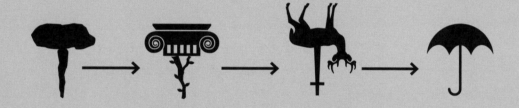

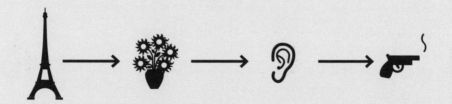

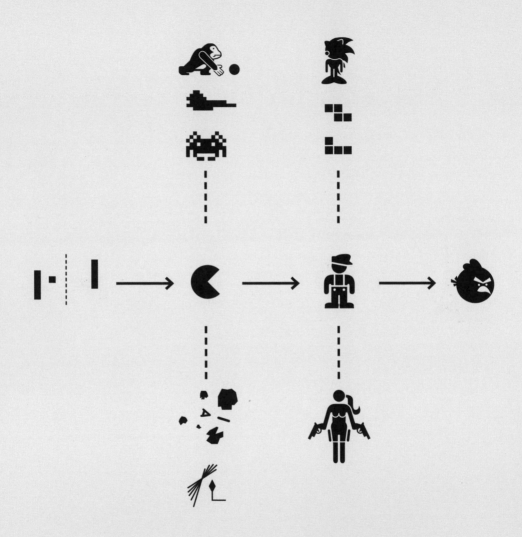

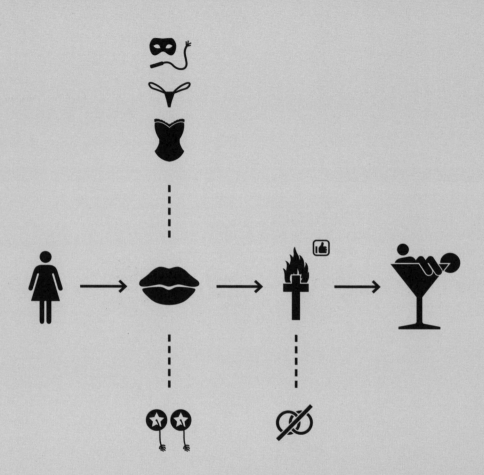

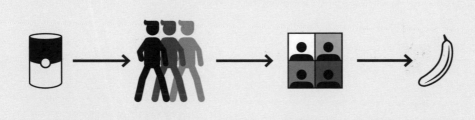

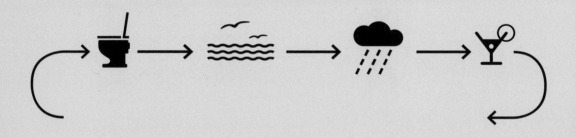

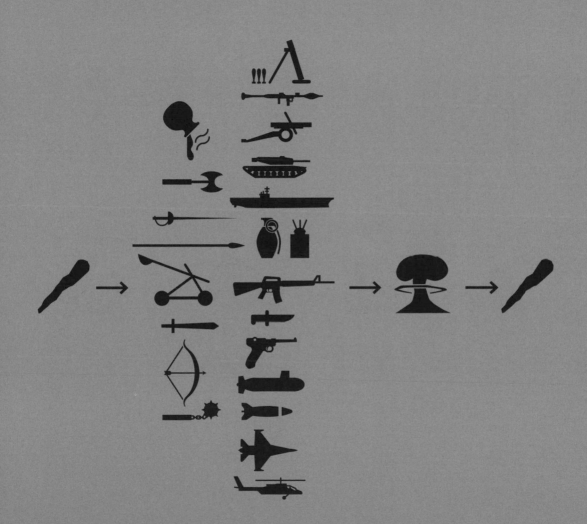

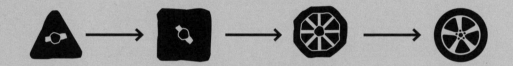

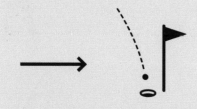

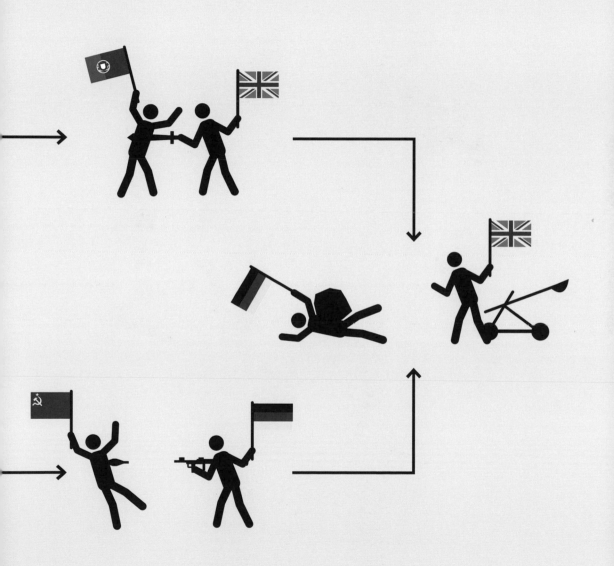

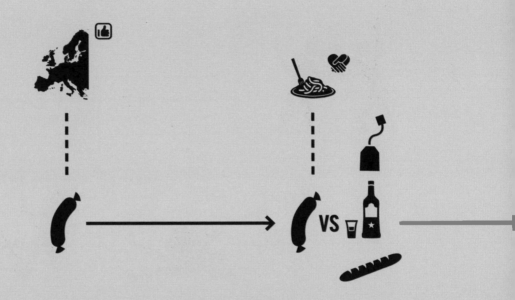

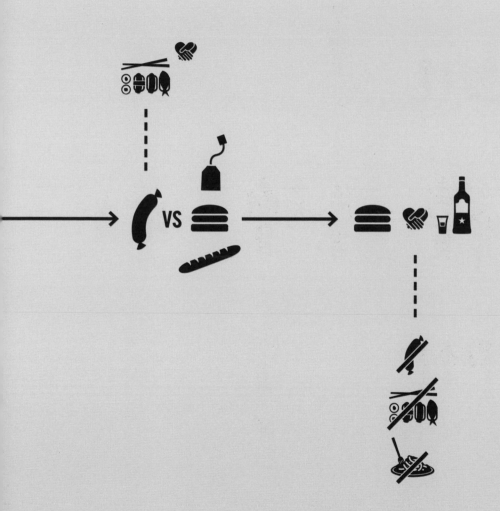

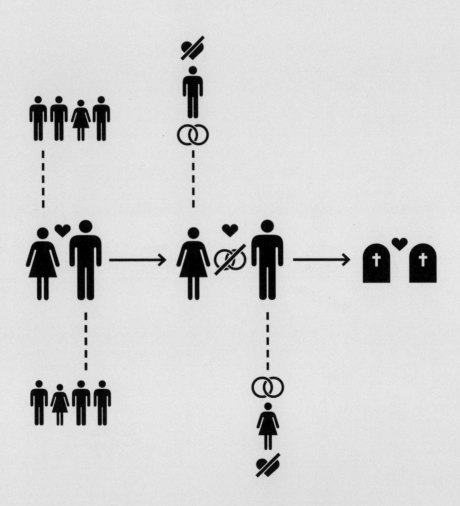

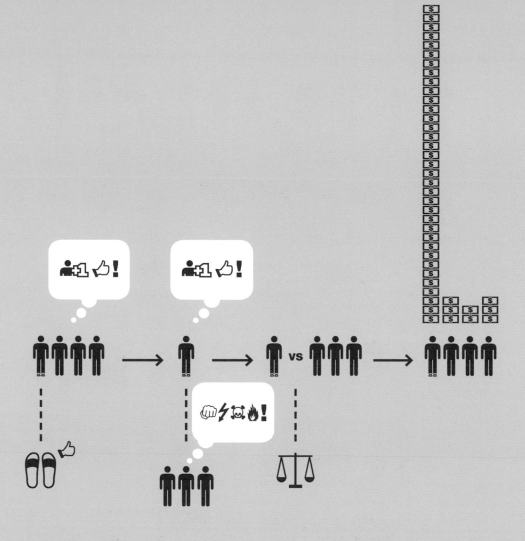

People

Animals

Vehicles

Sport

Cities

Objects

Food

TELL

YOUR OWN STORY

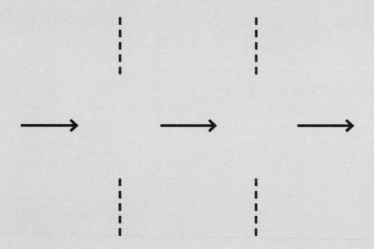

[   ]

Keep it simple. Summarize your life as much as you can. You just have to choose all the things that make you you. And remember: don't lie. Unless lying makes everything funnier.

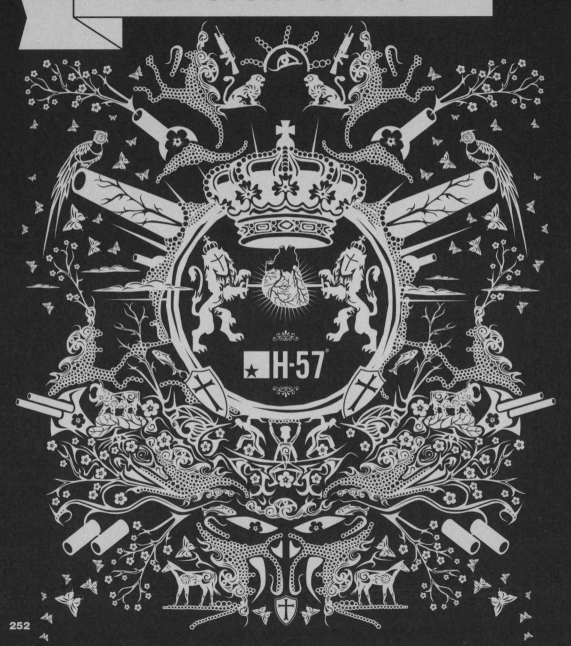

H-57 is a creative design and advertising studio based in Milan, Italy. Officially born on 12 January 2004, our name was inspired by the infamous Hangar 57, a legendary Russian Cold War base, the reality and whereabouts of which are both still mysterious, and which was said to house horrific weapons of mass destruction, a laboratory for crazy biological experiments and all kinds of secret and dangerous things.

In the beginning, living up to our name, H-57 achieved success producing provocative and menacing graphic T-shirts. We then found our true calling as a creative design lab, working on everything from graphic design to advertising, typography to illustration, animation to packaging. H-57 Creative Station was born.

Soon, H-57 began to collaborate with big agencies and international clients, including with Coca-Cola, Condé Nast and Lucasfilm, for whom we produced a series of typographic posters inspired by *Star Wars*, which went on to be sold for charity and the proceeds donated to Make-A-Wish Italy.

The stories in this book began life as a project to boil down issues of great historical importance into their component parts, using a series of individual graphics to tell a much bigger story. The result was six 'stories' (Marie Antoinette, Hitler, Michael Jackson, Jesus, Julius Caesar and Napoleon), which were posted online and quickly went viral. They came to the attention of a literary agent in London, who proposed that the stories be made into a book. And that book is what you have in your hands right now. If you bought it, we want to thank you. If you received it as gift, we admire your friend's taste. Please, tell them thank you from us.

The H-57 crew is made up of the three core people opposite, supported by a number of young collaborators, who are gifted with great talent and an equal amount of patience.

Matteo Civaschi

Matteo founded H-57 in 2004, together with Elena Borghi (who has since left), after 15 years working for big advertising agencies. Fond of music by Mozart and Van Halen, he is also a huge fan of science fiction films, from Ridley Scott's *Alien* to the world-famous, epic *Star Wars* saga by George Lucas. His three cats are his favorite assistants, especially during the nights when major projects come to life.

– – –

Gianmarco Milesi

In his early life, Gianmarco planned – in chronological order – to become: flute virtuoso, NBA player, guitarist and Egyptologist. That all went out of the window when he discovered copywriting, finding it to be a beautiful and entertaining job. After 12 years struggling along at large advertising agencies, he joined Matteo Civaschi at the helm of H-57. Upon retirement, he intends to become a flute virtuoso, NBA player, guitarist and Egyptologist.

– – –

Sabrina Di Gregorio

This mythological creature is part woman, part account handler and part whatever else you could possibly need. She was the first person to quit her previous job, accept the challenge and actually sit in the original H-57 office, back when the telephone didn't ring every 45 seconds, as it often does today. Legend has it that someone, somewhere in the universe, will one day manage to make her lose her temper.

h-57.com

- - -

- - -

firstfloorunder.com

THANKS TO

Thanks to Francesco Guerrera for his passion and friendship, and for the space he gave us on firstfloorunder.com.
This book is as you see it also for the talent and patience of Anna Barisani, who raised it with her hands. Brava Anna.
Nothing in H-57 would be possible without Sabrina Di Gregorio, a beacon in the night, a safe harbor every day and a merciless judge of our ideas.
Special thanks to Tim Glister and Will Francis at Janklow & Nesbit for believing in our idea every day, mail after mail. A great "thank you" goes to Jenny Heller, for her constant presence, enthusiasm and italian words. Grande Jenny. Our gratitude goes also to Ione Walder, and everyone else at Quercus, for putting order where there was chaos.
Thanks also to Nicola Lampugnani, Alessandra Miatello, Matteo Inchingolo, Alberto Aliverti, Monica Amigoni, Sabine Troisvallets, Orazio Marino and all H-57 friends on facebook and in all the other places, both physical and virtual.
A big hug to all of you.

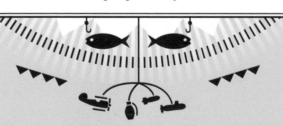

Quercus

New York • London

© 2013 by H-57

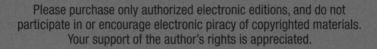
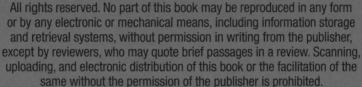
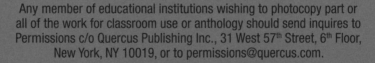

Any member of educational institutions wishing to photocopy part or
all of the work for classroom use or anthology should send inquires to
Permissions c/o Quercus Publishing Inc., 31 West 57th Street, 6th Floor,
New York, NY 10019, or to permissions@quercus.com.

ISBN 978-1-62365-012-4

Library of Congress Control Number: 2013937921

Distributed in the United States and Canada
by Random House Publisher Services
c/o Random House, 1745 Broadway
New York, NY 10019

Manufactured in China

2 4 6 8 10 9 7 5 3 1

www.quercus.com